FIRE SPOOK

MONICA GRAHAM

Phyllis -
Get spooked!
Monica Graham

Nimbus Publishing Limited
3731 Mackintosh St, Halifax, NS B3K 5A5
(902) 455-4286 nimbus.ca

Printed and bound in Canada

Interior design: Jenn Embree

NB #: 1054

Library and Archives Canada Cataloguing in Publication

Graham, Monica, 1954-, author
Fire spook : the mysterious Nova Scotia haunting / Monica Graham.
(Stories of our past)
Includes bibliographical references and index.
Issued in print and an electronic formats.
ISBN 978-1-77108-093-4 (pbk.)—ISBN 978-1-77108-094-1 (pdf)

1. Haunted houses—Nova Scotia—Caledonia Mills. 2. Ghosts—Nova Scotia—Caledonia Mills. 3. MacDonald family. 4. Caledonia Mills (N.S.)—Biography. I. Title. II. Series: Stories of our past (Halifax, N.S.)

BF1472.C3G73 2013 133.1'2971614 C2013-903458-7
C2013-903459-5

Canada

Canada Council for the Arts Conseil des arts du Canada

NOVA SCOTIA Communities, Culture and Heritage

Nimbus Publishing acknowledges the financial support for its publishing activities from the Government of Canada through the Canada Book Fund (CBF) and the Canada Council for the Arts, and from the Province of Nova Scotia through the Department of Communities, Culture and Heritage.

FSC www.fsc.org MIX Paper from responsible sources FSC® C103113

CONTENTS

The MacDonald farmhouse was located in the bottom quarter of this map, just below the dotted line that signifies the Antigonish-Guysborough County line.

INTRODUCTION

A GHOSTLY LEGEND

"There are more things in heaven and earth, Horatio, than are dreamt of in your philosophy." –Hamlet, *Act I, Scene V*

SPRING 2012: Snow melted peacefully from the dark trees, and dripped musically into the pools of water collecting along the trail to one of Nova Scotia's most remote and mysterious places. The guide pointed to a rocky, level spot covered with collapsed brown grass where Alex MacDonald's barn once stood. Off to one side sat the empty cellar of the famed "spook house," a shoulder-deep depression surrounded by a thicket of fir and spruce. Water filled a smaller hole nearby. Nothing else remained: not a sliver of charred lumber or scrap of scorched cotton to speak of the terror that filled the isolated home on January 11, 1922.

Ninety years after the fires that forced the MacDonalds from their home, the only evidence to prove the farmhouse ever existed is its overgrown cellar at the edge of a grassy clearing in the woods.

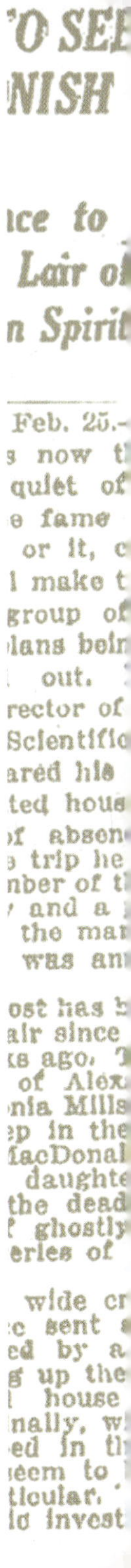
'O SEE
NISH
ice to
Lair of
n Spirit
Feb. 25.-
now t
quiet of
e fame
or it, c
l make t
group of
lans bein
out.
rector of
Scientific
ared his
ted hous
of absen
trip he
nber of t
and a
the mar
was an
ost has b
air since
ks ago.
of Alex
nia Mills
ep in the
MacDonal
daughte
the dead
ghostly
eries of
wide cr
c sent
ed by a
g up the
house
nally, w
ed in th
eem to
ticular,
lo invest

Today Caledonia Mills, *An Daigear* in Gaelic, is a string of homes, cottages, and farms scattered along the Guysborough Road. But when Canada was established in 1867, the community of 120 had a milling industry, a postal way office, and a school.

On that stormy evening, Alex and Janet MacDonald, their daughter, Mary Ellen, and their neighbours fought more than thirty strange fires that burst from the walls, ceiling, and furniture of their home. As fast as they could extinguish one fire, another blazed up somewhere else. After a night of firefighting, the MacDonalds moved out. The source of the fires was never discovered, but the Gaelic-speaking people around Caledonia Mills blamed *bochdans*, or ghosts. Soon the stories escaped the tightknit little community, making the whitewashed farmhouse on the hill the focus of international curiosity. The world heard tales of mischievous and unfriendly spirits that set fires, let the livestock loose, braided the horse's mane, and stole household objects.

When a Halifax newspaper offered a reward for solutions to the mystery, everyone had a theory. People blamed bochdans, vampires, demons, poltergeists, a nineteen-year-old curse, the then-unfathomable new technologies of electricity and radio, methane gas that crept silently from coal mines in the next county, illusions, and luminous phosphorous emanating from the soil. Maybe the American expert, Dr. Walter Franklin Prince, was right when he said that fifteen-year-old Mary Ellen set the fires while possessed by a spirit, or in a state of "altered consciousness."

Caledonia Mills

In the early 1800s William MacDonald and his family arrived in Antigonish County from Strathglass, Scotland. He took up land along the road from Antigonish to Guysborough, in the community of New Manchester Road Settlement. After he and his sons established a shingle mill, sawmill, kiln, and gristmills, the village changed its name to Caledonia Mills in a dual salute: to local industry and the ancient Roman name for Scotland.

After all, if a ghost could interfere with the respected journalist and tough-as-nails detective who investigated the mystery, then anything could happen to an impressionable teenager. Or maybe the international buzz simply arose from a lonely girl's quest for attention. If that was the case (and no one knows for sure), Mary Ellen got more than she bargained for; she later moved to Ontario and changed her name.

Photographs taken at the time show Mary Ellen beaming cheerfully as she stood among the neighbours, reporters, and psychic investigators who beat a path to her door, a difficult overnight trek by horse-drawn sleigh or wagon from the nearest town. The farm straddled the Antigonish-Guysborough County line, about two kilometres from its nearest neighbour and twice that distance from Caledonia Mills. The collection of farmhouses, grist- and sawmills, a schoolhouse, and a postal way office that

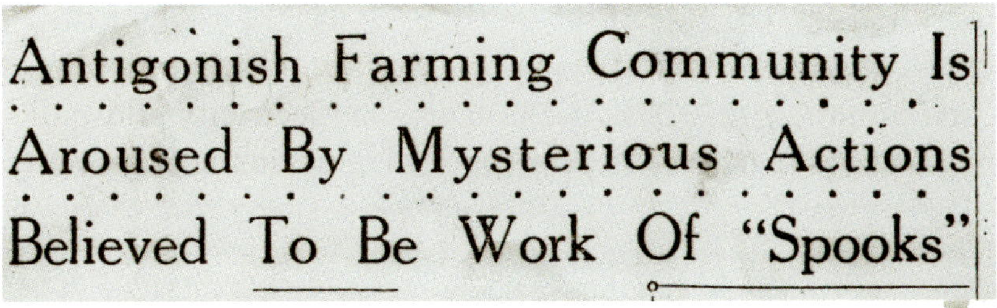
Antigonish Farming Community Is
Aroused By Mysterious Actions
Believed To Be Work Of "Spooks"

This headline appeared in the January 19, 1922, issue of the *Halifax Herald*.

Other Canadian Ghosts

While stationed in Sydney, Cape Breton, in 1784, British army officer Sir John Coape Sherbrooke saw the ghost of his brother Wynward whom, he later discovered, had died at that very moment. In the 1829–31 fire spook case in Baldoon, Ontario, John T. MacDonald's family and his fifteen-year-old adopted daughter experienced up to fifty fires a day (many started with bits of cotton), heard unexplained gunshots, and had rocks fired at them.

A rash of mysterious Canadian disturbances occurred between 1877 and 1891, including a poltergeist in Amherst, Nova Scotia, in 1887-89, and cattle escaping from their restraints at Dalhousie Mountain, Nova Scotia, in the 1890s. Fire spooks were recorded in Woodstock, New Brunswick, in 1887, and in Beaverton, Ontario, in 1891. A lull in ghostly activity preceded the Caledonia Mills fires, which started a new epidemic of psychic disturbances across Canada, including the 1943 mystery at the Hilchie home in Eastern Passage, Nova Scotia.

comprised Caledonia Mills was twelve kilometres along the old Guysborough Road from the village of St. Andrews. The nearest railway station was in the university town of Antigonish, fifteen kilometres northwest of St. Andrews and more than two hundred kilometres from Halifax. But the isolated location of the farm didn't prevent newspaper reports of fire-lighting spooks from captivating imaginations all over the world.

"Antigonish Farming Community Is Aroused By Mysterious Actions Believed To Be Work of Spooks," headlined the *Halifax Herald*. "The most weird, creepy and spooky mystery ever experienced in the Maritime Provinces," claimed the *Toronto Star*. As more people made the pilgrimage to Caledonia Mills, they embellished and spread the ghost stories, adding their own eerie experiences. Almost a century after the MacDonalds fled their home in distress, the tales still hold high entertainment value and continue to shiver spines at campfires and kitchen parties.

The mystery has attained legendary status, the historical facts lost or clouded with inaccuracies and exaggerations designed to frighten or intrigue audiences. However, the fires that forced the MacDonalds from their home in the winter of 1922 were well documented, as was the failure to satisfactorily determine what caused them. "It was the queerest thing I ever seen," one eyewitness summed up.

Alex, seventy, Janet, sixty-nine, and Mary Ellen MacDonald, fifteen, outside their home in 1922.

CHAPTER 1

THE MACDONALD FARM

The story began long before the 1922 fires. Alexander MacDonald was born near Caledonia Mills about 1851, at the home of his Scottish-born parents, John "Dhu" and Margaret MacDonald. Alex John Dhu, or Alex Black John, as he was known, and his brother, Dan, farmed the family property after their father's death in 1868, and lived in the family farmhouse.

In 1873 Alex married Janet Cameron. A year younger than her husband, Janet was one of eleven children born to John and Mary (Boyd) Cameron of New France, just twelve kilometres northeast of Caledonia Mills. In March 1887, Alex and Janet had a baby girl, Mary. A year later they moved into a one-and-a-half-storey wood-framed house that Alex built on the family farm, on the Guysborough side of the county line, in the Roman Valley electoral district. (A second house on the property was moved to the nearby Kenny farm about 1895.)

Just like most of its neighbours, the MacDonald home had no electricity, telephone, or running water, but it wasn't considered primitive by local standards. A solid structure of about nine by four metres, it had a dining room downstairs with a small wood-burning stove, a tiny bedroom, a parlour, an alcove just big enough for a bed, and a spacious kitchen addition with a big cooking stove, also fuelled by wood. Wallpaper covered the dining-room walls and the parlour ceiling, while the parlour walls and dining-room ceiling were brown-painted wood. Roll-up blinds covered the downstairs windows, and upholstered

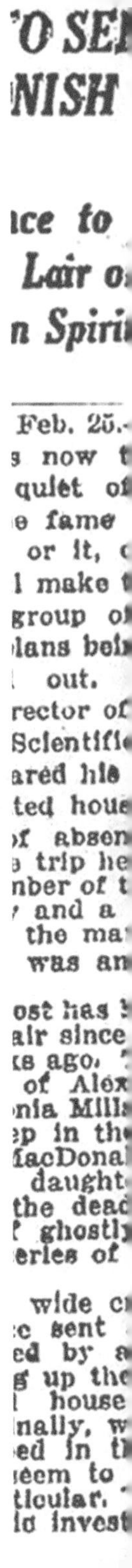

In 1922 fields and pastures surrounded the MacDonald house, part of the original property cleared for farmland by Alex's father when he emigrated to Nova Scotia from Scotland.

furniture beckoned the weary. Above the kitchen was a loft, while the second floor, over the main part of the house, served as a large bedroom, accessed by a stairway from the front parlour. A ladder led up to the kitchen loft, which had no opening into the second-floor bedroom.

A tall forest grew to the edges of the fields that surrounded the home, and, to the south and east, the Nova Scotia hills rolled towards the Atlantic Ocean. A livestock barn for the cattle, horse, sheep, and poultry stood north of the house, about thirty metres from the kitchen door, and smaller outbuildings containing firewood and farm equipment clustered around the house and barn. Alex, his father, his brothers, and most of the neighbours earned their living by farming as well as by cutting wood, with occasional trips outside the area to work for logging or mining companies, or at whatever jobs they could find.

By 1900 Alex's older brother, Donald Allan Dhu, had moved to Glace Bay in Cape Breton, while Daniel continued to farm part of

Nicknames

Nicknames related to geography, ancestry, or physical characteristics helped to identify people who had the same first and last names as neighbours or colleagues. Duncan Borrodale MacDonald's ancestors came from Borrodale, Scotland. *Dhu*, Gaelic for dark or black, identified John MacDonald by his complexion or hair colour; while his son became Alex John Dhu to avoid confusing him with other Alexanders. Likewise, Mary Boyd Cameron's use of her maiden name (Boyd) separated her from other Mary Camerons.

the original homestead. A third brother, Andrew, lived with family members between jobs at lumber camps across the Maritimes and in the eastern United States. Andrew never married, and he drank heavily when unemployed—which often coincided with his visits to Alex and Janet. Janet's mother, Mary Boyd Cameron, eighty-seven, also lived at the homestead at this time.

After her husband's death in 1885, Mrs. Cameron continued to live alone at the family home in New France, until she developed dementia. All night she called for her late husband. She roamed outdoors at all hours, forgot to eat, and sometimes didn't recognize her own adult children. Worried about her safety, her family closed the old homestead and moved Mrs. Cameron to the home of her son, Janet's brother, a few kilometres away at Frasers Grant. Her condition quickly worsened until the family could no longer care for her. They decided to place her in the County Home, also known as the Poor House, which opened in 1892 to care for the insane and destitute. County Home residents received little sympathy for their plight, but the Camerons had no other choice; the facility offered around-the-clock care for a sick, elderly woman with few options.

No one had asked for Janet's opinion. She was appalled to discover that her mother was in the County Home, and decided

County Home

The Antigonish Poor Farm and Asylum, also known as the County Home, opened in 1892 at West River near present-day Highway 7, the road to Lochaber. The third facility of its kind in Antigonish, it had no bathrooms, electricity, or entertainment at first. A hard-working supervisor, his family, a couple of nurses, and occasional hired kitchen hands provided basic care. Healthier clients helped raise the home's vegetables and meat, cook, clean, churn butter, wash laundry, sew, and care for disabled inmates. Many patients spent their days rocking on their beds and moaning, giving the facility a frightening reputation. Fire destroyed the home in the mid-1900s. A trailer park occupied the site in 2012.

that she would move in with her and Alex and their daughter. Alex opposed the plan, but couldn't dissuade his wife from bringing her mother to their home in the fall of 1899. Janet quickly regretted the move. Mrs. Cameron roamed, rarely slept, and screamed constantly for her dead husband. Janet began locking her mother into her small room at bedtime, but Mrs. Cameron quickly learned to escape by bumping her rear-end against the lock to lift the latch. Janet solved this problem by nailing the door shut, which confined the poor woman to ransacking the bedroom and wailing all night. Within months, Janet started tying her mother onto her bed. The County Home administrators and family members all refused to take Mrs. Cameron, leaving Janet to care for the invalid twenty-four hours a day, and still handle all the chores expected of a farm woman.

Janet reached her rope's end when, on April 27, 1900, Mrs. Cameron's ravings reached a new high while the family entertained visitors. Janet went into her mother's room to calm her, but nothing would work. Finally, Janet screeched: "I hope the devil in hell comes and takes you before morning!" A black dog chose that moment to appear from nowhere and walk through the kitchen into Mrs. Cameron's bedroom. No one knew where

Gaelic

Janet, Alex, and their daughter, Mary, spoke English as well as Gaelic, the tongue of their Scottish ancestors who settled in Nova Scotia in the 1800s. Despite government efforts to force everyone to speak English, about 50,000 people along Nova Scotia's North Shore and on Cape Breton Island still spoke Gaelic in 1901, including 75 per cent of the population of Antigonish County. With the language came a culture of storytelling, oral history, music, ceilidhs, and a strong connection between the natural and the supernatural.

The ancient language was discouraged as countrified and backward, but people continued to speak Gaelic at home while mastering English for the purposes of commerce and education. Gaelic largely disappeared from public use by the mid-twentieth century, when revival efforts included instruction in public schools and at facilities like the Gaelic College of Celtic Arts and Crafts at St. Ann's, Cape Breton, along with a focus on traditional music and culture. By 2012, the Nova Scotia government began to operate a Gaelic Affairs Office and organize student exchanges with Scotland.

the dog had come from, and no one could say where it went. But when Janet found her mother dead in her bed the next morning, everyone believed the dog had been a forerunner: a supernatural warning or omen of a future event, usually a death. (Years later, they remembered the dog as a sign of every sinister event that had happened at the MacDonald farm.) Despite the fact that she was eighty-seven and had been sick for four years, Mrs. Cameron's death aroused suspicions in the community. Neighbours wondered if she'd been "helped along" to the next world, especially when they heard that Janet had wished her mother to hell just hours before her death. Whispered allegations that Janet had smothered Mrs. Cameron were never proven or even investigated, but neither were they forgotten.

Until then, the MacDonalds had been known as a hospitable and generous family, in whose home neighbours

often congregated for card games and where supper was always shared. But after her mother's death, Janet appeared ever more bitter and withdrawn, and less welcoming. Some people thought she had a guilty conscience; others believed that the whispered accusations had hurt her feelings. Whatever the case, Janet had no patience for Andrew MacDonald's shenanigans when he arrived at his brother's farmhouse in the fall of 1903, flush with cash from a season's work in the United States and ready to party. As he swigged his liquor, cracked ribald jokes, and staggered around the kitchen arguing that he should have a share of the family farm, Janet's annoyance grew to match the ferocity of the rain and wind that howled outside the farmhouse. Finally she had enough.

"Out," she commanded Andrew, opening the door to let the gale swirl into the kitchen. "Get out—and don't come back."

Whatever Alex thought of his wife banning his brother from the home was not recorded, but Andrew's reaction is part of local folklore. As he went out into the November chill, he cursed his brother's family.

"*Théid do chur a-mach air an t-sitig air oidhche fada nas miosa na'n oidhche seo*," he said to Janet in Gaelic, which, translated into English, meant: "You'll be driven out on the dung-heap on a far worse night than this night."

Andrew spent the rest of the night at the home of long-time friend Duncan Borrodale MacDonald, regaling him with his account of his last evening at his brother's home. Duncan would

The Gaelic Curse

An Antigonish County saying, "Nothing worse than a Gaelic curse," reflects the emphasis given to words spoken in this tongue; Andrew's curse gained significance in later accounts because he spoke it in Gaelic. But in 1903, MacDonald kitchen conversation was in Gaelic, so it would have been unlikely for Andrew to curse in any other language.

Drummond Mine opened in Westville in 1867 as part of a Nova Scotia coal-mining boom that attracted country people, like Mary Ellen's birth parents, to the growing coal towns.

live to see the curse realized, Andrew predicted before leaving for Antigonish. Andrew's life spiralled downward until, completely destitute, he landed at the County Home. He remained there until he died at St. Martha's Hospital in May 1910, almost seven years after Janet had booted him off the farm.

For Alex, Janet, and Mary, life continued much as it did throughout the rest of rural Nova Scotia, governed by the seasons and demands of farm work. Neighbours' visits, the occasional ceilidh, and attendance at Roman Catholic mass in St. Andrews broke the routine of life in the Nova Scotia countryside. A trip to Antigonish or to one of the Pictou County coal towns was also a special treat. So when Alex found temporary work in Westville during the summer of 1910, Janet accompanied him so she could visit her friend, Annie, who had been widowed almost three years earlier.

Originally from Springfield, near Caledonia Mills, Annie Duggan married John Peter MacDonald, a relative of Alex and

Janet. The couple then moved to Westville, where John Peter found work at the Drummond Colliery. While labouring in the bottom of the mine shaft on October 13, 1907, a falling box of coal killed him instantly. John Peter's death was among more than six hundred Pictou County mining fatalities that occured

Mary Ellen's birth father's name, J. P. MacDonald, appears on the Westville miners' monument.

between 1838 and 1992. At the time of MacDonald's death, coal mine-labour strife filled Nova Scotia headlines, overshadowing reports of just one more miner killed in the dangerous pits.

Annie was left a widow with four orphaned children, including Mary Ellen. As Janet gazed at the round-faced four-year-old with the blue-green eyes, curly hair, and irrepressible grin, an idea came to her: Mary Ellen could live with her and Alex in Caledonia Mills. They would care for the child and make sure she attended school, Janet suggested to Annie. Mary Ellen would be company for them, now that their own daughter, Mary, was an adult and would likely leave home. The offer relieved Annie. She had already found a foster home in Guysborough County for her son, Walter, just a year older than Mary Ellen, but she still struggled to shelter, feed, and clothe the remaining youngsters on the meagre amount provided to her by community charities. If Janet took the busy toddler, Annie thought she could manage the care of her other two children, John and Anne.

Miners' Widows and Orphans

In 1907 widows and orphans, like Mary Ellen's birth mother and siblings, received financial help from deceased family members' workmates or union; from organizations like the Orange Lodge and Order of Odd Fellows, which cared for families of deceased members; from community charities; and, only occasionally, from the company of the deceased or the government. A miner might have, at this time, paid twenty-five cents a month into a fund similar to an insurance policy so that his widow could receive a seventy-dollar death benefit, and two dollars a week for two years.

Widows took in boarders, sewed, laundered, picked berries, sold garden vegetables, and worked at other stay-at-home jobs to support their families. They ran tabs at grocery stores and waited for their children to get old enough to find employment. Sometimes widows re-married, and commonly "farmed out" their children to be raised by friends or family. If completely destitute, widows and orphans were sent to the Poor House.

Mary Ellen lived five kilometres from the Caledonia Mills school; a long walk, which meant she often missed classes. The school opened in the mid-1860s and closed in 1957, when children in the community were sent to school at St. Andrews.

So Alex and Janet took Mary Ellen to Caledonia Mills as their daughter. The silence of the isolated farm bemused the little girl, who was accustomed to bustling Westville. There, her ears had been filled with the noise of pit-trains shunting all night, the chatter from thousands of miners as they changed shifts, the hiss of the pithead boilers, and the clanging and crashing from the blacksmith shops, coke ovens, and brick kilns. She had often been hungry and clothed in worn hand-me-downs, but there were always lots of people around. At Caledonia Mills Mary Ellen had only the company of the farm animals, Alex and Janet, both almost sixty, and their twenty-three-year-old daughter, Mary. Except for the wind in the trees and the birdsong, it was so quiet Mary Ellen could hear her heartbeat.

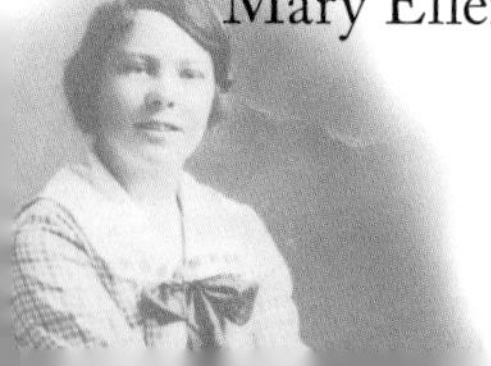

Soon after Mary Ellen's arrival, others also began to think the place was strange, but for different reasons. Weird things happened at the MacDonald farm. Visitors reported seeing balls of fire floating in the air, which one witness described many years later as resembling a burning beach ball. Strange noises plagued the house, both indoors and out, during which time anyone investigating couldn't open the door or breathe easily. Once the noise stopped, the door would open and breathing returned to normal.

On one occasion, visitors told of banging and roaring noises filling the house, followed by a loud crash when a set of china egg cups tumbled from a kitchen cabinet (they had been a prize at a card party at the farm some ten years earlier). A more sinister report involved a pet lamb found bleeding to death on the doorstep, its throat sliced. Household items like rugs and kitchen utensils went missing, laundry vanished from the clothesline, and a prized saddle disappeared from the barn—found later buried in the woods. Missing blankets were later found buried in the mud, and three rugs were found in the tops of the property's tallest trees.

On another occasion, Alex brought a new harness home from St. Andrews and locked it in the barn. The next morning, the door was still locked but the harness was gone. He asked around the neighbourhood, but no one had seen it. Some years later, he and a friend heard a cowbell in the woods where no cow should have been, so they went to look for the animal. After walking several kilometres without finding a cow, they sat on a fallen log for a rest. Alex noticed a metal buckle on the ground at his feet and gave it a tug; it was attached to his long-lost harness, buried beside the log. In the following ninety years, Caledonia Mills residents found other odd items, hooked in treetops or buried in the ground, which they believe had once belonged to the MacDonalds.

Neighbours first became aware of the disappearances about 1912–15, after Ronald MacGillivray found some rolled-up rugs

while checking his fences. Recognizing them from his visits to the MacDonalds, he took them to Alex, who commented that their dog must have carried them away. When MacGillivray found the MacDonalds' heavy iron pots on his property however, he knew the dog couldn't be responsible. It must be a bochdan, he suggested. A bochdan was as easy to blame as anyone else. The MacDonalds and their neighbours pondered the mystery until early 1921, when the dairy cows presented a new puzzle. While Alex might have previously suspected that Mary Ellen had carried off the missing kitchen items to play with them, she was in the kitchen with Janet the first time the cows got loose, in March 1921.

That March evening, after bedding all the animals down for the night, Alex heard a commotion outdoors. He investigated, and found that the four dairy cows had escaped from their stanchions and were wandering around the barn. The wooden stanchions consisted of two upright bars, just wide enough apart for a cow's head to fit between them. Two horizontal bars then held the cow's head in place, one passing above and one below the animal's neck, and fastened by sliding wooden pegs into notches. Assuming he'd forgotten to insert the pegs or that they'd worked themselves loose, Alex hammered them tightly.

The next morning the cows were loose again, so Alex used heavy nails to wedge the pegs into their slots. In the few minutes it took to carry the milk to the farmhouse and return to the barn, the cows had gotten loose again; so Alex wrapped haywire around the stanchions' uprights. But when Alex and Mary Ellen went to the barn later, four wandering cows met them at the door. Alex then moved two cows to another building where nothing interfered with them, but those left in the barn continued to escape. Even fastening chains around their horns failed to restrain the cows. Strangely, the beef cattle were undisturbed.

Tales of Alex's sneaky cows travelled throughout the countryside. Mary Ellen's classmates at the Caledonia Mills

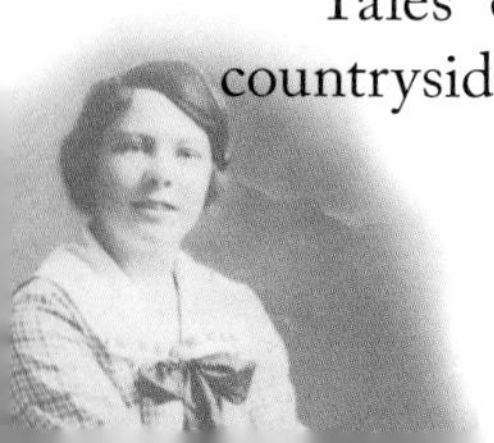

Jack "The Boxer" MacPherson (above) and his son, Alex, accompanied Richard Carroll to the MacDonald farm in March, 1921, and later hauled supplies to the farm for psychic investigators.

schoolhouse heard of bochdans meddling with Alex's livestock. By then married and living in Alder River, Guysborough County, Alex and Janet's daughter, Mary MacDonald Quirk, and her husband, William, discussed the situation with their neighbours. Later that month, some men from the nearby village of Beauly hitched up their horse-drawn sleigh and travelled over the hard, crusty snow to Caledonia Mills to cut fence posts and hunt game. On their way home late that afternoon, Richard Carroll, Jack "The Boxer" MacPherson, and his son, Alex, stopped at the MacDonald farm, where they accepted Janet's supper invitation while they waited for Alex to return from Antigonish. When he didn't come home by dark, the visitors offered to milk the cows and bed down the animals. Mary

A sketch by *Halifax Herald* artist Donald McRitchie shows the MacDonald homestead surrounded by snow during the winter of 1922. The inset drawing of Mary Ellen indicates her perceived importance in the Caledonia Mills mystery. "It was hard to see how the girl could reach the roof without a ladder," he told a reporter several months later. "If she did, she could hardly set the roof on fire with an ordinary match."

Ellen lit the way with a kerosene lantern, chattering about the neighbours' dislike for her parents. The surprised men asked why she thought such a thing. Someone played tricks on them by untying the animals, Mary Ellen explained. The men hadn't heard of the situation before, so they quizzed the girl. No matter what Alex did to restrain the cows, the next day they were loose, she said.

Alex still hadn't returned when his friends had finished their chores, so they went home. A riderless horse met them as they turned from the MacDonalds' lane onto the main road, a route that was in those days several metres closer to the homestead and within sight of the barn. The horse passed around their team and the loaded sleigh, and plodded on towards the MacDonald farm. The men figured it belonged to the MacGillivray farm next door. Glancing behind, they saw no horse, but a man walking away from them towards the MacDonald place. They hadn't met a hiker on the way down the lane. When they investigated some days later, no one had seen a man walking or a horse without a rider, and there were no footprints at all.

The men didn't keep the experience to themselves. Richard Carroll told the story to Alexander MacDonald of Antigonish,

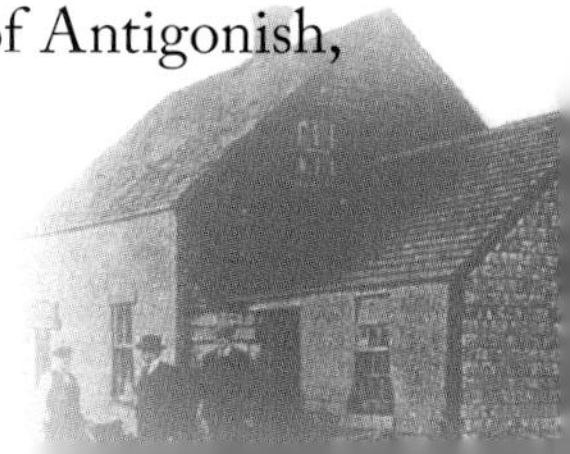

who recorded the conversation more than sixty years later in a typed account that survives to this day. The story told by Mary Ellen, along with the horse that turned into a man, was Carroll's first inkling of strange incidents at the farm, he told MacDonald. In the days before television, hair-raising stories about spirits, forerunners, and the second sight were entertaining pastimes. Well steeped in Celtic culture and its lore about spirits and the supernatural, many of the deeply religious residents of Antigonish County believed these types of stories. Some even mused that Alex had suspected his horse of fiddling with the cows when he sold it and bought a new one that spring.

The cows' "tricks" continued for two weeks, and then stopped as quickly as they had started, a situation attributed to the priest's visit. The young Cape Breton cleric apparently hurried away after the imprint of a horse's hoof suddenly appeared in a window frame, with no horse in sight. The mark disappeared in a few days—too late to repair the MacDonald farm's reputation. If unseen spirits frightened even the priest, what chance had anyone else?

Late that summer, a farmer and his son who were cutting hay near the MacDonald home saw flames rising from its roof. Hurrying to raise the alarm and fight a fire, they descended into a hollow where the house temporarily disappeared from view. When they reached high ground again, there stood the house: not a flame in sight. Fraser, the farmer, discussed the incident with his neighbours. They suggested that his imagination worked overtime, the sun had created an illusion, or even that glowing phosphorus rising from the soil had appeared as flames. As later events unfolded, other people from near and far would blame Mary Ellen, but none of these explanations satisfied Fraser.

In December the noise of rattling chains drew the attention of an Antigonish man passing Alex's barn in the wee hours of the morning. A faint, blue glow persuaded him the barn was on fire, so he rushed to the door to save the livestock. As he entered

the open door, the light disappeared. He left, believing his eyes had played a trick on him. That same December, another man saw a blue light in the barn as he passed by after dark on his way to Guysborough. He figured that either Alex was working late or the bochdans were busy; neither needed his help, so he left. No one knew it, but the MacDonald farm's curious events were about to evolve into terror.

A grainy photo from March 1922, shows (left to right) Alex MacDonald, Dr. Walter F. Prince, Leo MacGillivray, Dan MacGillivray, Harold Whidden, and Mary Ellen MacDonald, standing beside the kitchen addition of the MacDonald home.

CHAPTER 2

THE FIRES

Alex MacDonald's morning routine began at daybreak, while Janet and Mary Ellen huddled in their beds against the chill. He lit a fire in the kitchen stove, cleaned the lamps for the next evening, and went to the barn to feed and water the animals. By the time he returned to the house some forty minutes later, Janet and Mary Ellen would be bustling about the warm kitchen, which would, by then, smell of freshly cooked breakfast.

When Alex began his usual ritual that cold Saturday, January 7, 1922, he had no idea that his life would never be the same again. As he opened the stove to start the fire, he

Women's Work

Nova Scotia farm women cooked, housecleaned, and cared for their children. Typical tasks included gathering eggs; separating cream from the milk to make butter; gardening; harvesting vegetables, fruit, and berries; making jam and jelly; and salting meat for winter. They would also card and spin sheep's wool, which they would knit or weave into clothing. As soon as they were able, girls began helping with simple chores like picking dirt from sheep's wool, weeding gardens, sweeping floors, making beds, and cleaning the stove, before graduating to harder jobs. In a family with no boys, females also helped stack firewood, make hay, and care for the livestock. They toiled even harder when husbands and sons worked away from home.

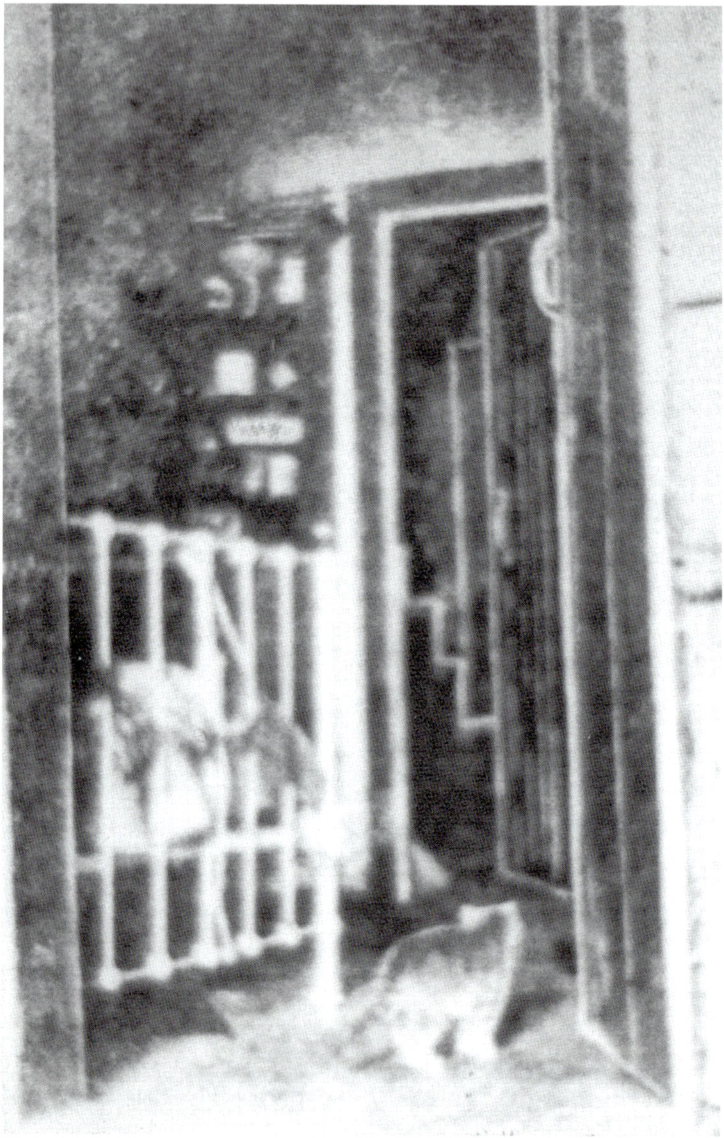

Mary Ellen's cat, Fluff, stands in the kitchen doorway facing the dining room, with a bed on the left. A cupboard can be seen on the far wall of the dining room and the stairs are visible through the door to the parlour.

discovered blackened bits of charred wood on its surface and on the surrounding floor. Knowing that the cinders couldn't have come from inside the stove, he glanced around for their source. To his alarm, he saw a deep, twenty-centimetre-long burn on the beam over his head and scorch-marks on two of the boards that rested on the beams that formed the floor of the kitchen. The scorched wood started a hand's-width away from the stovepipe and spread out almost a metre. He concluded that the kitchen fire had burned too fiercely, and had ignited creosote that had been collected on the inside of the stovepipe. The resulting flue fire had burned hot enough to make the nearby wood smoulder all night. The gap of untouched wood between the stovepipe and the beginning of the scorch-marks puzzled him, but a flue fire was the only explanation.

"Why didn't Chief bark?" he muttered to himself. "Not much of a watchdog."

Alex would have heard the dog if it had barked, because he slept in the small bedroom on the other side of the wall from the kitchen, where Chief was locked each night. Thankful that the fire had gone out without spreading, Alex vowed that it would never happen again. He took down the stovepipe, which went up through the loft to connect to a chimney and rested on a wooden platform in the peak of the kitchen addition. He scraped the tarry creosote from inside the flue and reassembled it, tidied up the mess, and lit a fire in the stove, as usual. The weather got warmer that afternoon, so the MacDonalds let the kitchen fire go out. Janet cooked a simple, light supper on the small stove in the dining room, which vented through a brick chimney built from the ground up through the roof. As a result, the kitchen stove was stone cold when they went to bed, a bit earlier than usual because Janet felt ill. An hour later, she came wide awake.

"Smoke!" Janet announced. "Alex! Something's burning."

Alex didn't move, assuming his frightened wife had imagined a fire because of the previous night's scare. But when Janet

said she heard fire crackling, Alex opened the kitchen door to see bright flames licking the ceiling and the loft above it. Alex slopped water over the fire to extinguish it, and then stayed awake to keep an eye on the embers. He doused four more fires in the loft before the sun rose on Sunday morning. Fearing that the chimney heat had ignited dust in the loft, the family took up each dry pine floorboard that Alex had placed loosely in the loft twenty-three years earlier, cleaned them, and put them back. Again that day, they let the kitchen fire go out during the afternoon. Alex even climbed up onto the roof to pour water down the chimney. Before they went to bed, all three inspected each room for fire hazards—a search that also proved no one else was in the house.

Despite the precautions, Janet smelled smoke about ten o'clock, a few minutes after everyone was in bed. Alex searched but found no fire, so he ignored her second alarm. Twenty minutes later Chief barked and Janet yelled, so Alex got out of bed and opened the kitchen door. Flames leapt from an upholstered rocking chair that sat about three metres from the stove. Alex grabbed it, shouldered through the kitchen door, and threw it into a snowbank. Upon returning to the kitchen, he saw a couch in flames on the opposite side of the room. He hauled it to the door and shoved it into the snow beside the chair. For the second night, Alex stayed awake until early morning, but no more fires would start that night, nor would they the following Monday or Tuesday.

Wednesday started normally. A January thaw melted the snow on the roof and the grey sky threatened rain. By late afternoon a light breeze rose from the south. Alex was working in the barn and Janet and Mary Ellen were puttering at the kitchen stove preparing supper, when Janet suddenly smelled acrid smoke. Nothing wisped from the stove, so she looked around. Nothing. She looked up to see one of the loft floorboards in flames. She climbed on a chair, grabbed one end of the loose board, yanked

it from the ceiling, and jumped down to throw it through the kitchen door. It landed in the wet snow beside the rocking chair and the couch. Before she tossed it outdoors, Janet noticed a scrap of cotton cloth stuck to the board.

"Strange," she thought. "I never saw that cotton when I swept the loft. I wonder where it came from."

Janet had barely formed the thought when another fire started in the loft. She and Mary Ellen slapped it out with wet rags, their screams bringing Alex from the barn. Thirty minutes later, flames sprang from the dining-room wall over the kitchen door. Alex threw a bucket of water at it, but not before it left a long, black scar on the wallpaper. He fetched a second bucket of water, just in case.

It was a wise move. Wednesday's fourth fire started in the wallpaper covering the brick of the dining-room chimney. The mild weather meant the MacDonalds hadn't lit the small stove, but its solid brick flue didn't leak, even with a roaring fire. Alex extinguished the leaping flames, but he had no time to speculate on the cause because another fire had blazed to life in the same room. A few minutes after dousing it with water, the MacDonalds discovered flames popping out of old cotton rags stored upstairs. They extinguished them and went back downstairs, only to find the wallpaper alight in the tiny bedroom off the dining room. The fire climbed up towards the corner of the room, scarring two walls from the floor almost to the ceiling. By that point, they feared the house would burn down and leave them homeless in the middle of a stormy night.

"Go to MacGillivrays' for help," Alex ordered Janet and Mary Ellen, referring to brothers Dan and Leo MacGillivray at the neighbouring farm, more than a kilometre away.

Taking a lantern, Mary Ellen and Janet rushed outdoors. They stopped briefly as the wind drove the heavy rain at their faces, taking their breath away and almost blinding them. They recovered and staggered through the knee-deep slush that

clutched at their feet. Bare tree branches whipped and clattered above them, and the lantern flickered in the angry wind. Finally, Janet stopped, out of breath and in tears. Age and recent illness had sapped her energy, and she couldn't keep up with Mary Ellen's determined dash through the woods. She sank into the soggy snow, her mouth open to suck air into her aching lungs, making her cough.

"You go on," she gasped at Mary Ellen. "Hurry!"

Mary Ellen plunged onward, the lantern waving wildly in her outstretched hand. "Help, help," she called. As she approached the MacGillivray home, she saw a figure in the open door, silhouetted against the light inside. She yelled louder: "The house is on fire! Help! Dan! Leo!"

Leo MacGillivray saw the lantern bobbing among the trees, but couldn't understand Mary Ellen's words until she drew closer. As she gabbled about fires and Janet collapsing on the trail, Leo and his brother-in-law, Duncan Borrodale MacDonald, drew on their coats and boots and dashed into the weather. Dan started to follow, but remembered the stove: what if his own house caught fire while he was fighting a blaze next door? He closed the draughts on the stove, and then harnessed the horse and sleigh, planning to bring Janet back to the MacGillivray home for safety. But when Leo and Duncan told Janet to wait for Dan to fetch her, she decided instead to go home.

As Leo and Duncan raced ahead, Janet and Mary Ellen struggled through the wind and wet. They reached the edge of the woods, about two hundred metres from the house, a full ten minutes behind the men. Mary Ellen left Janet and ran ahead to get Alex, who had spent his wife and daughter's forty-five-minute absence smothering flames. Alex left Leo and Duncan on fire-watch and ran to his exhausted wife. He and Mary Ellen half-carried, half-dragged Janet to the house, where she collapsed on a hard kitchen chair about the same time that Dan arrived with the horse and sleigh.

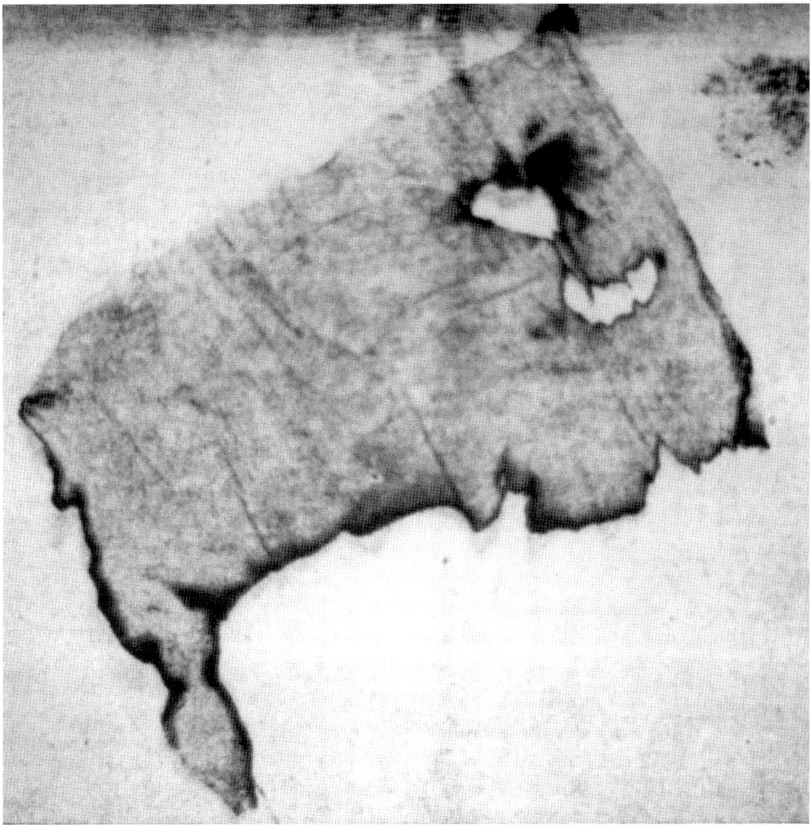

Evidence of the strange fires included this portion of the burned window blind in the parlour.

After checking every room, the group determined that no fires blazed and no arsonist hid in any of the corners. It appeared that the evening's fright was over. Revived by the notion that they were safe, Janet changed from her wringing-wet clothing as Alex stoked up the kitchen stove to boil water for tea. Dan declined food in order to return the horse to the stable, while the others ignored the house's damp chill and settled around the kitchen to discuss the night's events. Leo, sitting opposite the open door

between the kitchen and dining room, noticed the dog raise its head, hair bristling. Suddenly a bright white light silently filled the house, appearing from the parlour at the opposite end of the house. Leo jumped to his feet and dashed across the dining room to find pale-blue flames leaping from the green blind that covered the parlour window. He ripped the blind from the window and slapped the fire out with his hands. The flames singed neither Leo's eyebrows nor the hair on the backs of his hands, but destroyed all but the outside edges of the blind.

Leo, thirty-two, had lived next door to Alex and Janet MacDonald all his life, except for a few years when he had worked for an electrical business in Cobalt, Ontario. To him, the strange light looked like a short-circuit on a high-tension wire, but brighter. He searched the window and blind for a source of ignition, but was unsuccessful. "The fire was not very hot," he commented to Alex. "No," Alex agreed. "It was quiet, too. Lot of smoke, though."

The puzzled group returned to the kitchen, satisfied that the fire was out. But five minutes later they were on their feet again, this time to extinguish a fire in the still-wet wallpaper in the dining room. These flames glowed orange, and started in a completely different spot from the previous fires. All of a sudden, a calendar hanging in the parlour burst into flames. Although the calendar covered a stovepipe hole in the chimney, no fire had been lit in the parlour stove since the previous Sunday, so the flue was cold and dark. Fearing, again, that the house would burn down, Duncan ran back to the McGillivray farm to get Dan to telephone the neighbours to help fight the fires. Several people started to walk to the MacDonalds', but the stormy weather meant that they wouldn't reach the farm until morning.

The fires didn't wait. The bedclothes on a bed in the parlour ignited. After throwing water on the flames, they carried the mattress and other items either outdoors, or into the sodden dining room to keep an eye on them. Only the bed frame and

two pictures remained in the parlour. Then the dining-room wallpaper caught fire. How wet wallpaper could burn, no one knew. But if it could burn, it had to go—so Mary Ellen and Alex began scraping the wallpaper off with their fingernails. They scoured down to the next layer of newspaper glued to the wood as insulation, and scratched that away as well. As soon as they finished and went into the kitchen, flames burst from the exact place they just had stripped.

The wallpaper fires were followed by another fire upstairs, in a pile of cotton rags. After extinguishing them and heaving the scorched items outdoors, Leo and the MacDonalds went back to the kitchen, thinking they might get a break and have their tea. Just as Duncan returned with Dan, they smelled smoke and saw a bright light in the parlour. They ran to the other room to find a sofa cushion burning among the slats of the bed. "That was the strangest thing of all," Leo recalled a few days later. "We were all positive the cushion was upstairs…I saw paper burning when it was wet. I found pieces of cotton burning in the paper—that is, with the wallpaper and the newspapers behind the wallpaper—that was not there when I was there only a few minutes before."

They found cotton burning in a tiny cardboard box wedged behind a framed picture on the wall, and again in a Christmas gift box that everyone thought had been removed from the parlour. Flames burst from an empty pillowcase hanging on the dining-room sideboard; from a small piece of white cotton sitting on the bare table in the downstairs bedroom; and from a cotton sheet under the bed in the same room. They found tiny bits of cotton inside a cardboard raisin box and in two small baskets, which all caught fire separately, and in different parts of the house. The house reeked of burnt cotton, but no one recognized the fabric—mostly white with the occasional coloured piece. Someone picked up a piece of wet paper and put it on a table, where it caught fire. Leo and Mary Ellen witnessed flames ignite from a wet dishrag sitting in a puddle of water on the floor.

Arrows point to scorch marks on the dining-room wall caused by flaming wallpaper, while a dark mark in the corner indicates one of the worst flare-ups of January 11.

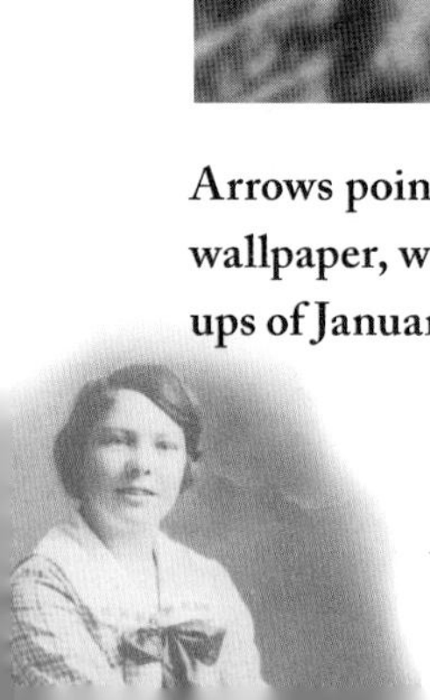

"There must be three inches of water on the floor," Leo said, as he stamped out the flames.

They couldn't figure out how the fires started, so they watched each other suspiciously as they stamped on and slapped at the flames—usually with their bare hands, because the fires were strangely cool. They soon realized that none of them would have had the opportunity to set the fires unseen, and no one could think of a motive for anyone doing so.

From suppertime Wednesday until eight o'clock Thursday morning, the MacDonalds and their neighbours had extinguished a total of thirty-eight fires. The sequence of the fires was blurred in their memories, but they pieced the evening together as best they could for the neighbours arriving that morning in answer to Dan MacGillivray's overnight alarm. The belated arrivals missed out on the fire-fighting action, but pitched in to help the MacDonalds move out of their home.

"If we don't get out of here, we might burn to death in our beds some night," said Alex. "Come stay with us," suggested Leo. "At least until you find another place." So, with the help of their neighbours, the MacDonalds packed their undamaged possessions into sleighs and hauled them to the MacGillivray farm. They left the scorched furniture sitting in the snow by the kitchen door, mute testimony to the events that drove them away.

The morning helpers included Michael MacGillivray and John Kenny, who had reached the MacDonald home on foot around ten o'clock. Their observation as they approached the house reinforced a growing community suspicion that supernatural forces had caused the fires. While still about ten metres away, they saw a bare forearm and hand extend through a window on the northeast side of the house, over the stairs. The hand waved a rectangle of white cotton cloth three times. They ran the rest of the way to the kitchen door to find the MacDonald family, Duncan MacDonald, and Alex and Colin MacIsaac packing household items. After greeting everyone, Michael took Duncan aside.

"Was anyone in the parlour just now? Is anyone else here?" he asked. "No, just us. We were all in the kitchen," Duncan replied. "Why?" Michael explained what they'd seen, so the men went quietly to the parlour stairs to look at the window, which was located over the stairs leading from the parlour. The glass was frost free, but there was no sign of a person or a cotton cloth. Dan MacGillivray's arrival with a team of horses to move the MacDonalds' possessions distracted them from their investigation. The men didn't tell Alex and Janet about the mysterious arm for fear of frightening them, but they later volunteered to swear under oath to the experience.

Alex MacIsaac and Leo experimented with lighting scorched bits of wallpaper with a match but, although now dry, the paper took a long time to ignite. Once lit, it extinguished almost immediately. The same thing happened when they tried to burn a piece of the damaged window blind. The men also searched for gasoline, kerosene, or other flammable liquids, but found none. They suspected that someone had set the fires, but who? The mysterious waving arm certainly seemed to pin the blame on bochdans.

The MacDonalds stayed with the MacGillivrays for three days, after which they moved into a vacant house near the main road. The rumours and gossip followed them. Within days, residents of Guysborough and Antigonish Counties trekked to the MacDonald farm to see the damage. Tongues wagged about the abandoned furniture sitting in the snow and mud, the scorched walls and ceilings, and the structural sturdiness of the home, despite the fires. Twice a day Alex visited the farm to care for the livestock, answering over and over the questions of curious visitors. When several people arrived at once, they discussed the mystifying events with each other, with witnesses, and with those who had heard the stories second- or third-hand. The county buzzed with information—much of it inaccurate.

Harold Whidden

December 29, 1888–January 13, 1970

Whidden worked as a sports reporter at the *Saskatoon Phoenix*, *Montreal Star* and *Halifax Herald* before joining the family business, G. B. Whidden and Sons. Following service in the First World War, he returned to Antigonish where he worked as an insurance agent before becoming the *Herald*'s Antigonish correspondant.

Four days later, on January 16, tales of a fire-setting spook at Caledonia Mills reached Harold B. Whidden in Antigonish. The word "spook," meaning ghost, had been in common English usage for about a century, and came from an early Dutch word for ghost: *spooc*. It sounded like front-page news to Whidden, the *Halifax Herald*'s Antigonish correspondent and its former sports writer. He queried his editor, who replied by return mail that Whidden should investigate the rumours and submit a story.

Whidden talked to Alex MacIsaac who, by then, was back at school in Antigonish after helping the MacDonalds move. Based on that interview, Whidden's first story appeared in the *Herald*'s January 19 edition. The same day the Antigonish newspaper, the *Casket*, published a brief description of the MacDonald family's plight. Thus began an international media circus that not only ensured the fame of Caledonia Mills and the MacDonald farm, but also affected all those concerned, including Whidden himself. If Whidden could have predicted the part he would play in the mystery, he might have steered clear of the whole subject.

Story Of "Spooks" Setting Fires In Antigonish Farmer's Home Confirmed

The January 24 *Halifax Herald* headline, now tattered and torn, that appeared after news correspondent Harold Whidden visited the MacDonald farm to see the fire damage for himself.

The story drew immediate reaction from *Herald* readers, far outshining public interest in the sorry news of a little girl whose frostbitten feet had been amputated after she wandered outdoors in her nightgown. Subscribers ignored labour unrest in Nova Scotia coal mines and the fierce winter storms that were playing havoc with train schedules. They wanted to read about the fire mystery.

Dennis assigned Whidden to visit the MacDonald farm for a full account, complete with photos. On the morning of January 20, Whidden and his friend Huntley MacNaughton left Antigonish by horse and sleigh, on the heels of a huge snowstorm. Once past St. Andrews, deep snow buried the fences and the men couldn't find the actual road. They followed tracks that were horse-belly deep, weaved through fields and farmyards, finally reaching Caledonia Mills in the early afternoon. They then left the team with Alexander and William Boyle and walked to the MacDonald homestead, which Whidden referred to as "the house of mystery." They followed the main road for more than a kilometre before turning onto a path through the woods. After wading through the deep snow for another two kilometres they reached the MacGillivray farm, where Dan offered to guide them.

Whidden described his first view of the house in the *Herald*'s January 24 edition.

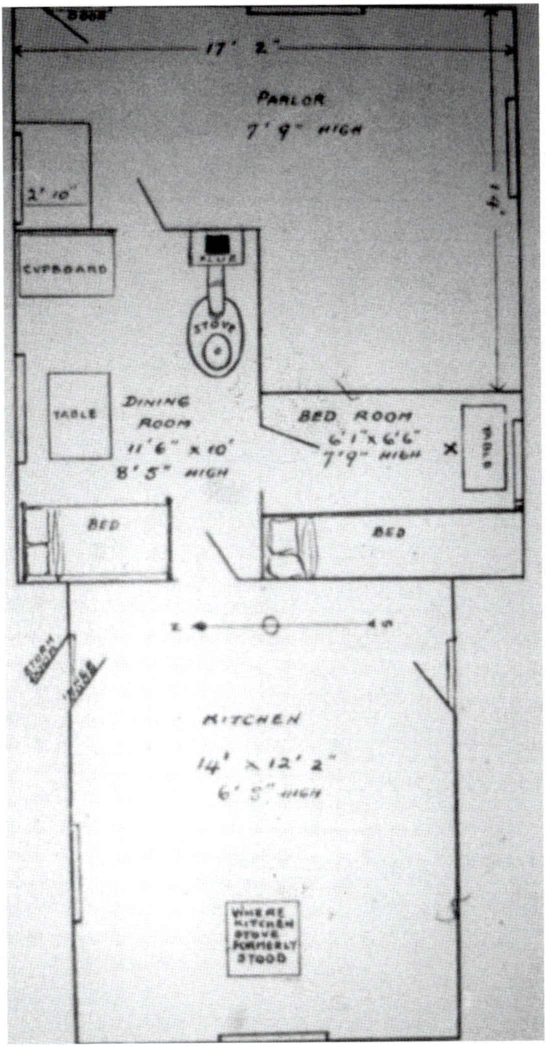

The floor plan of the MacDonald home demonstrates how people sitting near the kitchen stove could have seen through the dining room into the parlour. The stairs to the upper floor are on the top left, in the corner of the parlour.

On emerging from the woods the first thing that caught our eye was a small whitewashed house in a clearing, standing on a slightly elevated piece of ground....We found a sofa, or couch, by the side of the house, with a burnt place in the upholstering near the foot. Next we examined a dresser, which showed a distinct burn in the covering near the front.

Dan explained that a burning cotton pillowcase had damaged the dresser, and pointed out the big scorch mark on the back of the upholstered kitchen chair and several pieces of cotton that had been tossed into the snow after they had caught fire. Some were old rags of various colours, Whidden noted, but others were new, including an empty Robin Hood Flour bag. Inside the house, a "sorry-looking spectacle," the men noted the deeply charred ceiling beam in the kitchen and the burns in the loft floor, the scorched parlour window frame, and bits of burned paper still dangling from the dining-room walls. They examined sooty marks from sudden flares and numerous dark burns on the walls and floors, both downstairs and upstairs. The marks gave evidence to all the fires that Alex MacIsaac had described to Whidden, and more. The fires hadn't burned through the wooden walls; they had no connection to each other, the adjoining rooms, or to heat sources like the stove, the reporter noticed. He also noted that fire hadn't touched the upstairs ceiling, and that the home's basic structure remained intact. Further investigation showed there was no way a person could have snuck through the house unseen by any of the six people who fought the fires, nor was any fuel or other accelerant found on the premises. Whidden interviewed Alex, Janet, Mary Ellen, and the MacGillivray brothers, but couldn't speak to Duncan MacDonald because he wasn't home. Their stories all matched.

"We could not see how anyone could have started [the fires] under the circumstances...taking into account the way the house was laid off, its smallness, and the very fact that there was al-

ways someone in the house when the fires broke out," Whidden reported, concluding that "No one could offer an explanation, and the case remains a mystery."

Detective Peter Owen (Peachie) Carroll

CHAPTER 3

SEEKING SOLUTIONS

ANTIGONISH COUNTY RESIDENTS wrote to the *Halifax Herald* to tell its reporter to investigate the MacDonalds' trick livestock, including rumours about horses and heifers with braided manes and tails. When questioned, Leo told Whidden that the MacDonalds had indeed discussed the escaping cows with him, just five weeks earlier. It was true, Alex later agreed. Mary Ellen also told Whidden that she had seen the chained cows loose in the barn, and had helped her father put them back into their stanchions. However, no witness ever confirmed the horse and heifer stories.

Whidden's war service

During the First World War, Whidden enlisted as a gunner with Prince Edward Island's 8th Siege Battery, which went to England in 1916 and to France in 1917. Whidden sent regular reports to the *Charlottetown Guardian* from the battlefields of Armentieres, Passchendaele, the Somme, and Ypres; and wrote consoling letters to the families of his fallen comrades. In early June 1918, a mustard gas attack seriously injured him and killed most of the soldiers in his unit. After a year in a British hospital Whidden returned to Antigonish in 1919 to sell insurance and work as *Herald* correspondent. He married Clara Cunningham in 1923 and the couple had one child, who died young. A dedicated and lifelong community volunteer, Whidden died at Camp Hill Veterans' Memorial Building, Halifax. His obituary didn't mention his paranormal experience at Caledonia Mills.

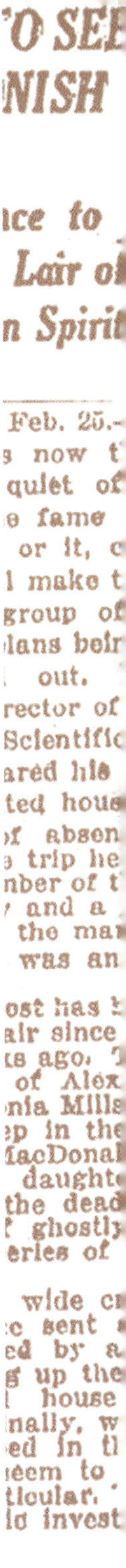
'O SE
NISH
ice to
Lair o
n Spiri
Feb. 25.-
s now t
quiet of
e fame
or it, c
l make t
group of
lans bein
out.
rector of
Scientific
ared his
ted hous
of absen
trip he
nber of t
and a
the ma
was an
ost has
air since
s ago.
of Alex
nia Mills
p in the
MacDonal
daught
the dead
ghostly
eries of
wide c
c sent
ed by a
g up the
house
nally, w
ed in t
eem to
ticular.
to invest

Eye-Witnesses Tell Of Mysterious Fires In Home of Antigonish Farmer

EO MacGILLIVARY and Duncan MacDonald, eye-witnesses to he mysterious fires which have curred in the home of Alexander acDonald a respected farmer at aledonia Mills, near Antigonish, ave confirmed reports of the fires lready published in The Herald.

In their interviews with Harold B. Whidden, The Herald representative, who visited the fire solely as a newspaper correspondent, they add to the mystery which deepens as the facts are brought out.

It has been suggested in Antigonish that detectives or scientists be sent to the scene of the "spookish" incidents to conduct a thorough investigation, which has puzzled hundreds who have already visited the MacDonald home.

Here is what the eye-witnesses say about the mysterious fires:

LEO MacGillivray, who gave his age as 32, said that he was born at Caledonia Mills, and that he had

LEO McGILLVARY

DUNCAN McDONALD

This January 25 headline appeared over Whidden's report from eyewitnesses Leo MacGillivray and Duncan MacDonald, and on the same page as the announcement of a contest to find the best solution to the mysterious fires.

The MacDonalds impressed Whidden who saw them as trustworthy but tired, with both their health and reputations endangered by the fires and surrounding gossip. Janet, who'd been running on her nerves during the fires and the move to their rented home, now admitted that the experience had exhausted her. Alex wondered aloud if the house would have burned to the ground if he'd just walked away from the fires. But the seventy-year-old told Whidden that he planned to build a new house, closer to the main road, and would continue to trudge back and forth to the barn every day to care for the livestock.

On Sunday Whidden and MacNaughton returned to Antigonish, where Whidden wrote his story and sent it to the *Herald*. "I wrote the facts given to me," he later recalled. "The case was so mysterious, and the circumstances were so weird, that I felt my position was unenviable. Therefore, both care and caution had to be exercised to write an accurate and straightforward story. There was not one word of exaggeration in it."

The people of Caledonia Mills either forgot or chose to stay quiet about their suspicions surrounding the death of Janet's mother twenty-two years earlier. As an outsider in the village, Whidden also didn't hear about Andrew's curse on the farm, although the incident would become pivotal to the story in the ensuing years. In 1922 local theories revolved around three basic points of view. Some residents blamed evil spirits, because they believed that the trustworthy witnesses to the fires would have noticed an arsonist. More skeptical people noted that a dishrag or paper soaked in alcohol and other substances would burn with a blue flame while appearing simply wet, and wondered why a spirit would need to use cotton to start a fire. A third group professed intense interest, but offered no opinions or theories.

"The stories gain interest with every recital," noted the Antigonish *Casket* on January 26. The *Herald*'s January 25 issue offered five-, ten-, and fifteen-dollar prizes to readers who provided the best solutions to the fire puzzle. Hundreds of replies from all over Nova Scotia poured in to the Mysterious Fires Editor. Some blamed fairies, demons, or witchcraft; a cushion pierced with a long pin would identify the culprit, who would feel no pain when sitting on it, readers advised. Failing that, a cow's heart stuck with pins and then boiled would somehow force a confession from the perpetrator. Alternatively, the MacDonalds could nail a horseshoe over the stable door to keep witches away. One man advised gaining insight from the *Book of Revelations*, and another suggested that the events had foretold the January 22 death of Pope Benedict XV.

The Contest

The January 26 *Halifax Herald* featured Whidden's January 25 story, describing his interviews with eyewitnesses Leo MacGillivray and Duncan MacDonald. Appearing in the same issue was the announcement of a contest put forth by *Herald* publisher William Dennis, offering prizes for the best solutions to the Caledonia Mills mystery. This move increased interest in the story as well as generating tips for Whidden, and investigations by Detective Peachie Carroll and parapsychologist Dr. Walter F. Prince.

One reader wrote several letters suggesting that a long-ago murder victim had turned into a vampire and returned to the crime scene in the form of fire, wind, animals, and people to force the current occupants out and reclaim the site. Several people suggested that someone had engineered the mysterious events to scare the MacDonalds into selling their land cheaply. The culprit wanted to farm the land or live in the house; access valuable resources like oil, coal, gold or pirate's treasure; collect on a reward for discovering the fire's cause; or simply wanted to cause mischief.

"If the fires started spontaneously, it must be due to chemical action," wrote a Mahone Bay schoolgirl, summing up several other submissions. She'd learned in chemistry class that phosphine could spontaneously ignite, and advised investigators to look for old-fashioned matches and ammonia from which the culprit could have made the substance. Phosphorus, used in marine signal-buoys because of its bright light when wet, was also suggested.

The Antigonish man who saw a bluish light in the barn in December said he believed someone with a blowtorch had been cutting the chains that secured the cattle, although the animals hadn't escaped since the previous spring. He also proposed that someone with plumbing knowledge had threaded small pipes from the kitchen stove through the MacDonald house in order

to make flames appear in odd places. Sparks from the wood stove ignited methane seeping from the ground, said a Yarmouth reader, while Antigonish-Guysborough school inspector Dr. A. G. MacDonald suggested that the house was a beacon for wireless electrical energy. Similarly, chief engineer I. Edward Spedding from the Dominion Coal Company's ship, SS *Wabana*, proposed that wireless electrical currents from generating stations had overloaded the atmosphere. The electrical tension found its way to the ground at the MacDonald property, igniting stray bits of cotton. Since the stations worked harder at night, that's when the fires were more likely to occur, he theorized. He didn't say how the strange cotton had arrived at the farm, but other readers proposed that rodents had used it for bedding. Some pointed to the cotton that wrapped household electrical wiring, ignoring the fact that the MacDonald home and its neighbours didn't have electricity until the 1940s.

If the devil started the fires, "where in hell did he find the cotton?" questioned one respondent. Another reader answered: a ghost took it from a coffin lining. "Let someone else adopt Mary Ellen for a while," read one submission. Panicked Nova Scotians feared an arsonist was at work, and that their own homes might be next. The MacDonald family couldn't occupy the house, nor could they collect insurance because the building still stood. The resulting financial hardship called for investigation. Insurance underwriters demanded satisfaction, predicting that other home-owners might torch their buildings, blame ghosts, and then collect the insurance. They wanted the provincial fire marshal, Major J. A. Rudland, to find the source of the mysterious fires. Rudland, busy with a Lunenburg case, asked his Antigonish County deputy to investigate the Caledonia Mills fires. Before the deputy could act, Dennis decided to hire a professional—a move that gave his newspaper exclusive control of the story. He contacted several prominent detectives who all turned down the job. They included Sir Arthur Conan Doyle, the author of the

Peachie Carroll

Both Detective Carroll and psychic investigator Dr. Prince and his team arrived at the Antigonish railway station before travelling to Caledonia Mills by horse and sleigh, the only possible means of transportation in 1922.

A policeman since 1884, Peachie Carroll enjoyed his reputation as a charming adventurer and unpredictable rogue, an image that served him well in his search for criminals. His friendly and leisurely exterior hid the agile mind and physical power of a tough detective, whose chosen method of investigation usually involved interrogations disguised as friendly interviews, the constant veiled threat of punishment, and a dogged search for clues.

Although sixty-two and nearing the end of his career when he took on the Caledonia Mills case, Carroll could still easily intimidate law-breakers and mischief-makers with a well-placed word or stare. The MacDonald farm investigation was his last big case, although he continued working for another few years before retiring. He died in 1933 after a lengthy illness, in his hometown of Pictou.

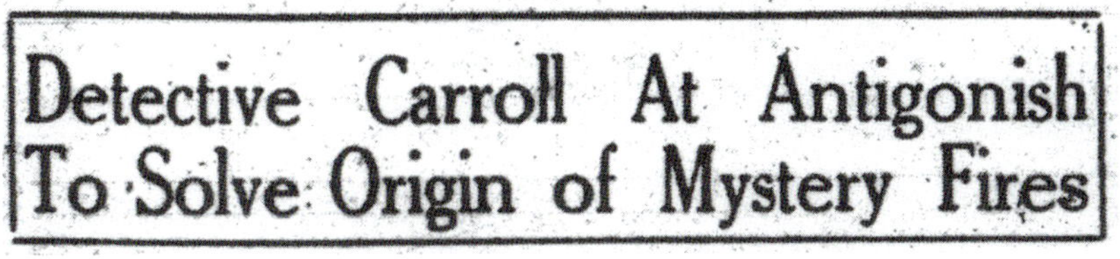

Detective Carroll At Antigonish
To Solve Origin of Mystery Fires

Peachie Carroll fully expected to solve the fire mystery, and arrived armed with unspoken hunches announced in this February 3 *Herald* headline. He discarded his theories when he began to investigate the case.

popular 1880–1914 Sherlock Holmes detective stories; and Chief Detective Horace Kennedy of the Nova Scotia Provincial Police.

"Please don't ask me to mingle with spooks," Kennedy pleaded. So Dennis hired the popular and flamboyant detective Peter Owen "Peachie" Carroll, who was based in the town of Pictou, about eighty kilometres west of Antigonish. Carroll was a former police chief in the Nova Scotia towns of Pictou and Yarmouth, and in Nelson, British Columbia, and was also a member of the provincial police. He secured his reputation with the arrest of a man involved in the 1892 murder of a New Brunswick policeman, and was equally feared by moonshiners, poachers, and thieves. Luckily for Dennis, Carroll was between cases in early 1922 and agreed to investigate the Caledonia Mills mystery. With Rudland's approval, Carroll went to Antigonish, arriving on the February 2 noon train.

Although reporters in the Halifax newsroom drew straws to see who would travel to Antigonish to cover the story, the assignment fell to the local correspondent, Whidden. He met Carroll at the railway station, where the detective told him not to expect a quick solution to the mystery. "I intend to wind this business up as soon as possible," Carroll said, however. "If I can do it in a day, so much the better. If not, I will follow my campaign through in every detail. Perhaps the case will be much easier than I anticipate. It may even be much more difficult. I do not know."

Carroll booked a room at the Royal George Hotel, and invited Antigonish Police Chief Colin MacLean to meet him for a chat about the case. Neither man recorded the conversation, but it became clear that Carroll sought background information on all the people involved. Afterwards, MacLean told Whidden he expected Carroll would ferret out the truth.

"If the fires were caused by human agencies, he is the man who will produce the evidence," MacLean said, adding that he'd not visited the scene personally and that his information was second-hand at best. The community wanted an official examination of the case, mostly to halt gossip about the MacDonalds, a well-regarded family, he said. "I am glad the case is being investigated."

Carroll interviewed other people in Antigonish that day, including a man and a woman implicated by letter-writers as being responsible for the fires. The suspects remained unidentified, but popular opinion held that they were local sorcerers said to cast evil spells. Carroll's interviews with both characters gleaned nothing, except that the community suspected them because they were eccentric. Carroll privately told Whidden that he began to suspect the case might be the most difficult in his career, even though he'd first suspected a single person had perpetrated all the strange events. He didn't name his suspect or say how he expected to expose the culprit, but confessed that nothing so far supported his hunch, which was based on second-hand information. "The whole thing is more mystifying to me than when I came to Antigonish," Carroll said in a conversation reported in the *Halifax Herald*.

Since the evidence gleaned in Antigonish was confusing rather than enlightening, Carroll decided to go to Caledonia Mills. He and Whidden planned to stay there as long as it took to investigate suggestions from *Herald* readers, and to prove or disprove Carroll's own theories. The men left Antigonish on the afternoon of Monday, February 6, with a horse hauling a

Alex's ladder (left), which he used when pouring water down the chimney to prevent fires, still leaned against the roof in this photo of the MacDonald house, barn, and outbuildings as they appeared in the winter of 1922.

large delivery-sleigh piled with enough food for a week, buffalo robes, a sheet iron stove and stovepipe, kitchen utensils, an axe, and a typewriter—all the necessities for camping and writing in the abandoned MacDonald house. Treacherously icy roads slowed their progress, which reached a crawl when they ran into a snowstorm about twelve kilometres short of Caledonia Mills. With snow blocking the main road and darkness closing in, the men led the horse by flashlight across the fields. At half-past seven they reached the Boyle farm, where they stayed the night.

The next morning Carroll and Whidden walked to the MacDonalds' rented house so the detective could interview them. They told their story, reiterating that they had no idea how the fires had started, and were certain no one could have lit them without being seen. Alex complained that a lot of rumours circulated about the farm, but was adamant that the fires and escaping cows were the only strange events ever to take place there. He promised to help Carroll and Whidden in any way he could, because he wanted the gossip to stop. Carroll had hoped the family would move back into their house with their belongings in order to replicate the circumstances in which the fires took place, but changed his mind when he discovered that Janet was too ill with

a bad cough to return to the house. Making her sicker wouldn't help anyone, Carroll decided.

That evening Carroll, Whidden, Alex, and Duncan MacDonald went to the vacant farmhouse, joined along the way by Dan MacGillivray. They installed the stove in the dining room and lit a fire to warm the damp building. They used hay from the barn to make deep layers over the floor, where they built makeshift beds from buffalo robes and blankets. Leo MacGillivray arrived later that evening, and left with his brother Dan about midnight. Alex MacDonald curled up in the rugs on the hay to sleep, while the other three men stayed up all night playing cards, fuelled by strong coffee.

Throughout the evening, Carroll conducted a long, gentle interrogation of the witnesses assembled at the farmhouse. He drew information from them so gradually they barely realized it, while Whidden took notes for the stories he would get someone mail to Halifax each day. No strange fires started and no ghosts appeared, but Carroll confirmed that all the witnesses told the same story.

The next morning a snowstorm arose as Alex fed and watered the livestock, so he and Duncan decided to return to their families while they could. The storm raged across the hillside all day, howling around the house and piling snow against it. Unable to see further than three metres through the drifting snow, Carroll and Whidden huddled over the stove. They closed the doors to the rest of the house to contain the heat in the dining room, but the stove's meagre warmth escaped through gaps between the boards where the wallpaper had been peeled away.

The men took turns trying to sleep, but cold air swirling across the floor kept them awake. With no expectations of any ghostly experiences that day, they considered moving to one of the neighbours' homes, but stayed put because they might easily get lost in the storm. Whidden's story wouldn't make it to the post office that day.

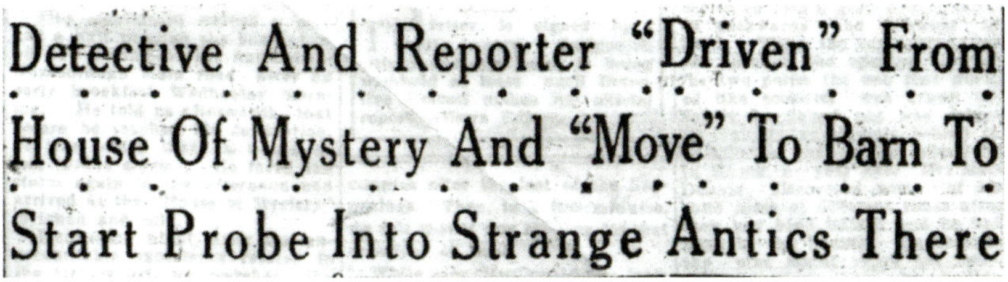
Detective And Reporter "Driven" From House Of Mystery And "Move" To Barn To Start Probe Into Strange Antics There

A February 14 headline in the *Halifax Herald* describes Carroll's investigation of the escaping cows.

Carroll broke the monotony with periodic explorations of the house, each foray followed by a session by the stove to attempt to get warm. He examined closely all the burn marks that had been reported, and found a few that no one had yet described. He took away the scorched sheet from under the bed in the downstairs bedroom, which he kept for years as a souvenir. Following suggestions mailed to the *Herald*, he looked for evidence of gasoline, alcohol, and other flammable agents, as well as mechanical, electrical, or chemical devices that could start fires. He found none.

By late afternoon the wind calmed a bit. The men looked out to see Alex wading through waist-deep snow towards the house. Exhausted, shivering, snow-covered and sneezing, he came in and joined the detective and the reporter by the fire. He had almost gotten lost in the snow, he told them, adding that he was coming down with a cold. But he'd brought them some of Janet's homemade stew, which Carroll and Whidden happily devoured. "Everyone we have met in Caledonia Mills has been kindness itself," Whidden reported in the *Herald*'s February 10 issue. "They are anxious to have the mystery solved and are rendering every assistance."

As darkness fell, the snow ended and stars popped into the night sky. Duncan MacDonald and the MacGillivray brothers arrived, armed with a load of firewood for the night. They played

forty-fives until about 10:30, when Duncan and the MacGillivrays went home under a rising full moon. Alex lay down to sleep, next to the wall that separated the dining room from the kitchen. Whidden followed suit an hour later, picking a spot about a foot from Alex. Carroll sat wrapped in his overcoat by the stove, puffing on his pipe and thinking about the conversations he'd engineered with the witnesses under the guise of friendly chit-chat. By midnight the peace had almost lulled him to sleep, until sudden noises over his head startled him to wakefulness.

Carroll listened carefully to the distinct sound of someone walking across the floor over his head, in the empty room upstairs. Without extinguishing the lantern and candle that sat on the table, he stealthily moved from his chair to the hay, hoping that whoever made the noise would assume all the men were asleep. His action woke Whidden, who mumbled something. The overhead footsteps started anew. "Did you hear that? Someone walking up there?" Whidden hissed, now wide awake and sitting up. Carroll nodded yes, placing his forefinger in front of his lips to tell the reporter to keep quiet. As they listened, the footsteps descended the stairs and moved into the parlour, and then...nothing.

The whole episode lasted about six minutes, followed by no sound but Alex's breathing. The men sat for a while and then Whidden pulled the rug over himself and curled onto his right side, with his right hand under his head and his left arm extended along his left thigh, under the heavy blanket. As Carroll lay down, he felt an impression on his left wrist as if someone had touched him. At the same moment, Whidden jumped.

"Did you hit me?" he demanded of Carroll.

"No," Carroll replied in surprise. "I did not hit you."

"Someone slapped me," Whidden said. "Just above my left elbow."

The men looked around them. There was no way that either Carroll or Alex, who was still asleep, could have touched

Mystery At Caledonia Mills Deepens As Detective and Reporter Get "Slap"; Search House In Vain With Flashlights

The reporter and detective became part of the mystery when they experienced otherworldly contact in the middle of the night, described in a February 4 story in the *Herald*.

Whidden without being seen. Moonlight poured into the room, so any movement would have been detected.

"I didn't imagine it," Whidden said.

"No," agreed Carroll, telling him about the pressure on his own wrist.

Whidden felt a strange presence in the room but, just to make sure Alex hadn't slapped him, he awakened the farmer. No, he hadn't struck the reporter, nor had he heard the footsteps upstairs. Whidden stood and removed his fur-lined overcoat. "I wonder if it left a mark on my arm," he muttered, as he doffed the sweater that he wore under the coat. He also removed an inside jacket and two shirts, to reveal no mark on his upper arm. "It didn't hurt, but I felt it distinctly through all my clothes," he explained to his companions.

The men took their flashlights and searched every nook and cranny in the entire house, upstairs and down, but found no sign of anyone. Fifteen or twenty minutes later, Whidden said he felt that whatever had caused the noises and touched them was now gone. They couldn't sleep, so they sat by the stove, feeding it wood and listening expectantly. The outdoor temperature plunged to minus thirty-three degrees Celsius, one of the coldest nights of the year. Alex complained of a sore throat, and

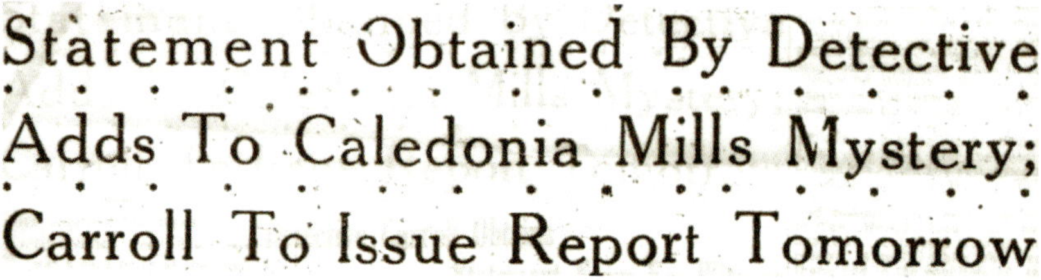
Statement Obtained By Detective Adds To Caledonia Mills Mystery; Carroll To Issue Report Tomorrow

The February 15 *Herald* headline refers to the hand waving the white cloth through the window, seen by Michael MacGillivray and John Kenny. The men's statement created an additional mystery that was never solved.

Whidden began to sneeze and sniff. It was half-past four before they slept, and only then for a few minutes. "A more desirable breeding place for pneumonia can scarcely be found," Whidden observed in his newspaper report.

After a miserable night, Carroll and Whidden arose early to make breakfast while Alex did the farm chores. Upon discussing their investigation, they decided it was too dangerously cold to stay in the house while both Whidden and Alex were ill. Also, the storm had prevented Mary Ellen from joining them, which Carroll considered important to the investigation. If they needed to return to study the case further, they would do it in better weather, they decided. Before they left, though, they carried out a careful examination of the house, from the cellar to the roof. Both men were certain that frost cracks, which occur in a building when the temperature drops quickly, hadn't caused the strange overnight noises.

Whidden went upstairs and walked back and forth while Carroll stayed below to listen. The footsteps sounded almost identical to the noises of the previous night, allowing for possible differences between Whidden's weight and gait and that of the person responsible. There was no way for anyone to get past them to or from the parlour stairs without being seen, and a solid wall separated the kitchen loft from the upstairs bedroom.

The exterior door to the parlour remained nailed shut and the windows tightly closed, just as when Carroll and Whidden had arrived at the homestead. The floorboards and shingles didn't rattle, discounting another theory for the noise in the night. After breakfast Alex showed them the barn and other outbuildings, pointing out the stanchions that had failed to hold the dairy cows. It was humanly impossible for anyone to have unfastened the cows in the few minutes he was absent from the barn, he told Carroll.

The men again visited the MacDonalds so that Carroll could ask Mary Ellen and Janet more questions. He also questioned the man who'd seen the blue light in the barn, and interviewed other unidentified people. Carroll impressed Whidden with his tact and cunning in extracting information from witnesses without their realization. But what Carroll learned did not help the investigation, or prove the unspoken hunch he'd had upon his arrival.

Accompanied by Dan MacGillivray and Duncan MacDonald, Carroll and Whidden packed the sleigh and hitched the horse for the return journey to Antigonish. The snow was so deep that it took three hours to reach the Boyle farm, less than four kilometres away. Dan and Duncan shovelled through the drifts that reached the horse's neck. Carroll and Whidden stayed overnight at the Boyles' place again, where the neighbours gathered for a card game and send-off ceilidh.

The two men left the Boyles' at nine in the morning to face snow that at times hid the telegraph poles. Along the way they stopped at the local post office so Carroll could interview Michael MacGillivray who, with John Kenny, had seen the arm waving a white handkerchief through the window on the day they went to help the MacDonalds move. While there, they collected Whidden's second missive to the *Herald*, which Leo MacGillivray had carried six kilometres to the post office only to have it sit there because of the blizzard. They stopped at St. Andrews for lunch and then went on to Antigonish, arriving

Offer Two-Hundred-Dollar Reward

WE, the undersigned, Peter O. Carroll, of Pictou, Nova Scotia, and Harold B. Whidden, of Antigonish, Nova Scotia, do hereby, EACH offer a reward of $100.00 to the first person who can prove conclusively, within one year from this date, that the unfastening of Alexander MacDonald's cows, in his stable at Caledonia Mills, in the County of Guysboro, in March, 1921, was effected by any agency other than supernatural or preternatural.

And also that the mysterious fires in the house of the above mentioned Alexander MacDonald, which occurred between the 11th day of January, 1922, and the 12th day of January, 1922, were set or caused by any agency other than supernatural or preternatural.

This offer is open to everybody.

Signed: P. O. CARROLL.
Signed: HAROLD B. WHIDDEN.

Antigonish, February 14.

Statement by Detective Carroll

P. O. CARROLL'S summary of the mysterious case—the happenings in the house and barn of Alexander MacDonald, Caledonia Mills:

After what I consider A THOROUGH INVESTIGATION, which included a careful examination of Alexander MacDonald, his wife, and adopted daughter, Mary Ellen MacDonald, the MacGillivray brothers, Dan and Leo, Duncan MacDonald and Mike MacGillivray;

After examining the house and barn carefully, and seeing WITH MY OWN EYES the scars of the fires, some of them charred, others scorched, and others more like smooches caused by fire;

And after spending two days and two nights in the house, I FIRMLY BELIEVE that neither the fires nor the other strange happenings were the work OF HUMAN HANDS.

Signed: P. O. CARROLL.

Antigonish, February 14.

Carroll and Whidden's offer of a two hundred-dollar reward appeared in the February 16 issue of the *Halifax Herald*, right above Carroll's investigation conclusions.

there at suppertime. That evening, Carroll wrote his professional conclusion in which he briefly described his investigation.

"After spending two days and two nights in the house, I firmly believe that neither the fires nor the other strange happenings were the work of human hands," he said, before dating and signing the report.

Whidden and Carroll put their money on their findings. Right above the conclusion, printed in the February 16, 1922, issue of the *Halifax Herald*, they promised a two hundred-dollar reward to the first person who could prove them wrong within a year.

The March 11, 1922, *Halifax Herald* ran Bryce Climo's composite image of Mary Ellen and Whidden standing at the MacDonald farm (bottom right), with inset photos of (left to right) Leo MacGillivray, Alex MacDonald, Dr. Prince, and Dan MacGillivray.

CHAPTER 4

A PSYCHIC TURN OF EVENTS

The *Herald* story, which ran on the same page as the challenge, was headlined "Detective Carroll, Baffled, Unable to Solve Mystery Fires At Caledonia Mills." Carroll didn't admit that the case had stumped him. He did say no human had lit the fires and fiddled with the livestock. Those who disagreed with Carroll's conclusion were free to form their own opinions, but first they should gather some facts, he said.

In issuing their public challenge, Carroll and Whidden appeared confident that no one would prove them wrong, either because they knew the culprit or culprits and took steps to keep it secret; because Carroll believed if he couldn't solve it, no one could; or because he genuinely believed that ghosts had done the dirty work. It certainly appeared that Carroll's aim was to stop the finger pointing and gossip surrounding the case, as he often declared his sympathy toward the MacDonalds' plight. No evidence cast suspicion on the people of Caledonia Mills, Carroll said, warning readers against making unfounded accusations.

Both Carroll and Whidden denounced claims that the situation made a laughingstock of Antigonish and of Nova Scotia. It was no joke to be driven from home in mid-winter for no apparent reason, they pointed out. "These people are just as innocent of this affair as I am myself," Carroll said sternly. "If anyone dares to point the finger of accusation at any one of them in this matter, I hope they would be made to prove it

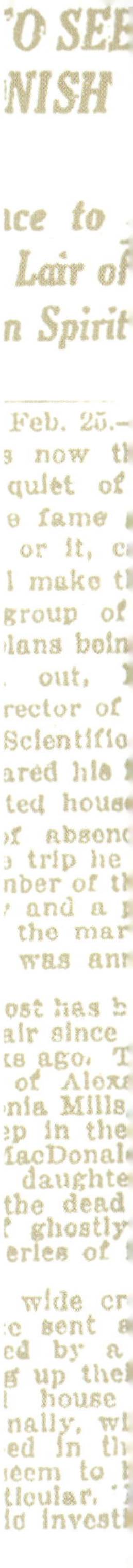

legally or swallow their words." Carroll thought his conclusion would end the fuss and the MacDonalds could return to their quiet country life, maybe in a different house. He was wrong.

The spook story grew wings. By March 6, 1922, Whidden's reports made the front pages of prominent newspapers around the world. The *Vancouver Sun*, *Toronto Star*, *Montreal Star*, *Kansas City Journal*, *New York Tribune*, *Boston Globe*, *Chicago Herald-Examiner*, and the *St. Louis Star* all ran stories about the weird events at the Nova Scotia spook farm, also known as the "mystery house." Editors contacted *Halifax Herald* publisher William Dennis for information and when they couldn't get it, they made it up. Dates, names, and the details of Carroll's investigation were exaggerated or invented. According to fabricated reports, the heifers' tails were braided; the horse had been ridden into a lather; Carroll and Whidden stayed at the house for two weeks; and Carroll had handcuffed the devil, who slipped away to leave the cuffs burning hot. The people of Antigonish and Guysborough Counties, including some who helped feed the tall tales to foreign reporters, came to resent the lies and the mockery, and closed ranks against further questioning.

But everyone wanted more information. Parents complained that Carroll's endorsement of the ghost stories scared their children; the wireless theory caused business headaches in the radio industry; and researchers seeking scientific explanations for unusual events wanted details. With Carroll's murky conclusion of the investigation, publisher Dennis saw room in the field for another kind of expert. Of all the ghost-hunters who contacted the *Herald*, the American psychic investigator Dr. Walter Franklin Prince seemed the candidate most likely to get answers.

Prince, a well-educated, self-described skeptic with a background in theology and social work, had already solved some mysteries labelled by the—then new—scientific term, "paranormal." After reading Whidden's report in an American newspaper, he wanted more information for the American Society

Dr. Prince

Walter Franklin Prince (1863–1934), an Episcopalian priest from Boston, studied theology at Drew Theological Seminary and Yale University, where he earned a Ph.D. in 1899. He ministered to several congregations and lived in a haunted house, experiences that piqued his interest in parapsychology.

The study of paranormal events was not considered to be truly scientific, but it was a subject examined by the American Institute for Scientific Research, which Prince joined in 1916–17. At that time it was taken over by the British-sponsored American Society for Psychical Research. Prince became research director in 1920, but left in 1925 to establish the more scientific Boston Society for Psychical Research. Prince, a skeptic and critic of fraudulent psychics, wrote several books and investigated a number of paranormal cases.

of Psychical Research. When he offered to investigate free of charge if someone would pay his expenses, Dennis couldn't refuse. Prince arranged leave from his work at the society, and exacted a promise from Dennis to keep media and onlookers away from the farm in order to maintain scientific objectivity. Dennis agreed, no doubt pleased that Prince had just handed the *Herald* exclusive access to the story. Prince arrived in Halifax on March 4—too late to receive the *New York Times*'s offer of a huge sum for exclusive story rights to his findings. Headlines screamed that a scientist planned to solve the mystery after everyone else had failed, and that the Antigonish ghost was about to be disturbed. With every re-telling of the story, Caledonia Mills faded further away into the hills and the ghost got bigger.

Prince promised to study the case and present his unbiased findings and the reasons for them, regardless of public opinion. Dennis agreed that the newspaper just wanted the paper to get to the root of the matter. Despite his vow of objectivity, Prince mused publicly that he expected to find poltergeist activity inspired by the Great Amherst Mystery of 1878–79. In that case, fires, moving furniture and flying household items had disturbed

SCIENTISTS TO SEEK ANTIGONISH GHOST

Dr. Walter Prince to Lead Invaders of the Lair of Eerie Canadian Spirit.

HALIFAX, N. S., Feb. 25.—A party of inquisitive scientists now threatens to break in upon the quiet of the Antigonish ghost, whose fame grows with each new thrill he, or it, causes. The exclusive wraith will make the acquaintance of a small group of quite distinguished men, if plans being discussed today are carried out. Dr. Walter Franklin Prince, Director of the American Institute for Scientific Research, New York, has declared his intention of calling at the haunted house if he can arrange a leave of absence. If the American makes the trip he will be accompanied by a member of the Montreal Spiritualists' Society and a professor of science from one of the maritime provinces universities, it was announced today.

The Antigonish ghost has become quite an international affair since it first was heard of a few weeks ago. The haunted house is the home of Alexander MacDonald, near Caledonia Mills, in a little-inhabited valley deep in the mountains and woods. Mr. MacDonald, his wife and their adopted daughter fled the place in terror in the dead of Winter with weird tales of ghostly tampering with cattle and a series of inexplicable fires.

The tale obtained wide credence and the provincial police sent a detective. He was accompanied by a newspaper man, the two taking up their residence in the MacDonald house for three nights, fleeing it, finally, with an eerie tale of being slapped in the night by hands that didn't seem to be attached to anything in particular. Now comes the call for scientific investigation.

A February 26 Boston newspaper announces Dr. Prince's intention to investigate the Caledonia Mills mystery, and describes the community as a "little-inhabited valley deep in the mountains and woods."

the Teed household of Amherst, Nova Scotia. Prince believed that Esther Cox, a relative of the Teeds who had been staying with them, had a second personality that had committed the mischief. He suspected the same kind of activity at Caledonia Mills.

Halifax City Police assigned Detective Reyno to accompany Prince in the hunt for clues, and to arrest a culprit if found. But no detective accompanied Prince when he took the March 6 train from Halifax to Antigonish. His entourage included Harold Whidden, the *Herald*'s photographer, Bryce Climo, and its artist, Donald McRitchie.

Upon arriving at Antigonish early that afternoon, Prince, Climo, and McRitchie booked into the Royal George Hotel. The

Herald staffers began amassing supplies and finding transportation to Caledonia Mills for early the next morning, while Prince snooped. He studied Carroll's report, interviewed Whidden at length, and pored over his newspaper reports about the fires. "Fiery Ghost of Antigonish Won't Perform for Science" shrieked a headline that continued, "Eerie Flame Sprite That Burns Water and Sets Mysterious Blazes Maybe Afraid of Dr. Prince." Dated March 4, two days before the expedition reached Antigonish, the writer pretended a close relationship with the investigation and quoted Prince as saying "There ain't no such animal [as a ghost]," an unlikely turn of phrase for the scholarly researcher.

Halifax Herald artist Donald McRitchie

The unidentified report, which survives to this day as a photocopy of unidentified origin, included a lengthy—and embellished—version of the MacDonalds' experience with the fires. The account was just one of many sensationalized and invented news items to infuriate Prince. Before leaving for Caledonia Mills on Tuesday, March 7, he prepared a statement for the next day's *Herald*. In it, he stated his disappointment that widespread public interest meant that he couldn't work in peace up until his final report at the end of the investigation. To counteract rumours and tall tales, he promised daily updates on his progress.

Before leaving Antigonish, Prince met with Rev. Dr. H. P. MacPherson and Rev. Dr. J. J. Tompkins of St. Francis Xavier University, and with Antigonish-Guysborough school inspector, Dr. A. G. MacDonald, to ask them for their opinions on the situation, and for character assessments of the people he would meet in Caledonia Mills. Carroll had followed similar steps, but with Police Chief MacLean instead of clergymen and professors. Dr. MacDonald, who continued to advocate his theory that wireless radio energy caused the fires, loaned Prince a heavy fur coat for the sleigh ride into the country. Prince's top hat and suit jacket were inadequate for the conditions, he informed the American.

The men left Antigonish at 8:30 A.M., taking three sleighs over crusty snow. One sleigh held their provisions and bedding and the other two carried the passengers. As the day progressed, the snow softened, the sleighs sank further into the drifts, and Prince became chilled despite the fur coat. They stopped first at the MacDonalds' rented home, where they received a cold welcome. Tired of enduring jeers and stares, the family initially resented another intrusion. But when they discovered how far Prince had travelled and realized he took their plight seriously, their Highland hospitality asserted itself. They agreed the men could move into the farmhouse for a couple of weeks. Alex said he'd accompany them, as he visited twice daily to care for the livestock. Prince persuaded Mary Ellen to come along, but Janet refused to join the expedition.

The entourage continued to the farm, with Prince remarking on the lonely wilderness of spruce and fir along the way. Alex and Mary Ellen reached the farmhouse first by way of the footpath, and helped warm the house and prepare it for the night. The men brought the sodden and weathered furniture in from outdoors and placed them in their original positions. They built a fire in the stove to diminish the damp chill and settled in to solve the mystery. Prince planned to sleep in his clothes, so that he could rise quickly should anything strange take place. Otherwise, he told the group, he expected everyone to behave normally. While two of the reporters cooked a hot supper, Prince explored the house. That night Leo MacGillivray visited, and told his story yet again.

Dr. Prince's group left Antigonish on March 7 for Caledonia Mills. Prince, wrapped in a fur coat, sat in the lead sleigh, followed by a sleigh piled with provisions, and with a third for Climo, McRitchie, and Whidden.

The expedition then settled down for the night, a wild one with rain pelting on the windows and wind howling in the eaves. According to an American newspaper that interviewed Leo MacGillivray by telephone, Prince strung small bells through the farmhouse to alert him to nighttime movement. Despite weather similar to the fiery night of January 11, the bells didn't ring. No fires, strange noises, waving arms, roaming animals, or mysterious taps on arms disturbed the disappointed occupants. The investigation would be thwarted if nothing happened during their stay, because it would be the only real evidence Prince could collect. Nothing remained of Carroll's and Whidden's experiences but their memories, and the scorch marks were the only evidence of fire. Prince didn't give up hope, though. If nothing happened the second night, he planned to change the conditions at the house to attract an event. "They intend to

Poltergeist

The German word for noisy ghost, "poltergeist" is the world's most well-known pattern of psychic phenomenon, involving knocking and tapping, moving or throwing objects, and possibly featuring water and fires. It seems to take place most often in the presence of young people, especially teens who experience repressed anger or sexual tension. Some theories claim the otherwise unexplained events are the result of psychic energy held by the teens, sleight-of-hand tricks, or acts of Satan.

carry on the investigation 'til the Caledonia poltergeist is either banished from his accustomed haunts or scientifically classified," assessed the *Casket*.

Prince soon discovered that the house stood firmly, despite its age and two months of emptiness. Except for the blizzard, the wind had blown little during Carroll's investigation. The wind whistled constantly during Prince's tenure, first from the southeast and then from the north, but nothing rattled or shook. The stairs and the floors didn't creak, the roof shingles remained tight, and the windows fit well. Prince concluded that the wind had not caused the strange noises heard by Carroll and Whidden, and concurred that it would have been difficult for someone to sneak around unnoticed.

On March 9, a few days into their occupation of the farmhouse, McRitchie and Whidden agreed to Prince's suggestion that they undergo a psychological test to break the monotony. McRitchie went first. Prince spread pages of foolscap over the dining-room table and asked the artist to relax and hold his pencil over the paper. Then Prince addressed any spirits in the room, telling them this was an opportunity for them to communicate. Nothing happened. Then it was Whidden's turn. Prince thought Whidden might be psychic, because of his experience in the house with Carroll. But, just as Whidden expected, nothing happened.

(Left to right) Donald McRitchie, Dr. Walter F. Prince, and Harold Whidden standing outside the MacDonald home in March 1922

It rained hard all day on Friday, March 10, so the men stayed indoors, reading, writing, and sketching. That afternoon, Whidden volunteered to try the psychological test again, if Prince had time, but the arrival of Mary Ellen and Janet by horse and wagon interrupted the experiment. Prince made changes each day in hopes of attracting psychic or paranormal events, and Janet was Friday's addition. "This made the family circle complete," Whidden reported.

Dan MacGillivray, who owned the nearest phone, arrived during suppertime to tell Whidden that the *Herald* had telephoned to speak to him. Whidden didn't want to leave in case something happened in his absence, but after talking it over with Prince he told Dan he'd visit the MacGillivray home closer to 7 P.M. Prince went into the small downstairs bedroom to read, while Whidden sprawled on the bed in the dining room to finish his cigarette. Suddenly, something prompted him to rise. He went to Prince, touching him on the shoulder. "Would you mind giving me that test again?" he asked. "If it's convenient."

Whatever Prince saw in Whidden's face made him agree immediately. He cleared a small table in front of the bedroom window, where a candle burned on the sill. Whidden laid out a few sheets of paper, sat down, and took his mechanical pencil from his vest pocket. He held the pencil point over the top-left corner of the paper, with his arm and hand resting easily on the table. He looked away from Prince, who sat on his right. Suddenly pins and needles tingled through the fingers of his right hand, until it became numb. The pencil began to move slowly, of its own volition.

After almost a minute, the pencil began to form slow circles on the page, then moving faster until Whidden's hand whirled over the paper. The tip of the out-of-control pencil ripped through three sheets of paper at a time, covering six pages with circles, and then a seventh with slanted lines. On the eighth page the pencil moved erratically, stopped for a moment, and then began making large, sloppy letters.

"McRitchie," Whidden yelled hoarsely. "Come see this. You may never see this again in your life." By the time McRitchie, Janet, Mary Ellen, and Dan came running, the moving pencil had already etched words onto the paper. Then, the energy that had apparently taken over Whidden's hand began to control his mouth, and ordered Prince to ask certain questions.

"Ask who set the fires in Alexander MacDonald's house," Whidden demanded, as he scrawled the same words on the paper.

"Do you know?" Prince asked.

Yes, wrote the pencil.

"Can you tell?" Prince asked.

Dr. Walter Franklin Prince (centre), with Alex (left), and Mary Ellen (right) are shown at the MacDonald farm in March 1922

Spirits! An exclamation mark punctuated the immediate answer.

"Why?" Prince asked.

The question appeared difficult to answer. The pencil circled and tapped fiercely on the paper, producing dark blotches and breaking the lead. McRitchie handed another pencil to Whidden, who scribbled random words.

"Everybody, be quiet! Get out of the room!" Whidden shouted wildly. Only Prince stayed, watching Whidden's pencil tapping and scribbling. It began to write an answer to Prince's question, but didn't complete it. So Prince asked a different question.

"Did you slap Harold Whidden on the arm the second night he and Mr. Carroll were in the house?"

Yes, was scrawled on the paper.

"Why?" asked Prince.

The answer, complete with exclamation mark: *Because I wanted to show him that the mystery fires were caused by spirits!*

Dr. Prince asked why the spirits caused the fires, and then asked the spirits' names. The surprising answers were scrawled on the sheets of paper, accompanied by information that Prince and Whidden had never heard before.

"Who unfastened Alex MacDonald's cows?" next appeared on the page, before Prince asked the question.

I did!! followed, punctuated with two exclamation marks and underlined six times.

For more than two hours Whidden hunched over the table, his face at times a nose-length from the paper. He used up page after page as Prince re-sharpened the four available pencils and McRitchie fetched more and more paper. At times Whidden's hand snaked out involuntarily to clutch Prince and draw his attention to the pages. When Prince couldn't sharpen the pencils fast enough, Whidden used broken bits of graphite to scribble messages; one message came from his sister Florence, who had died ten years earlier. Among messages of kindness and sympathy was a part that read: *People must realize that those who have passed beyond are ever present. God is merciful. God is good. He is just...Spirits do visit the Earth after death.* The writing then promised no further troubles for the MacDonalds, and that they would never see the spirit. Finally Whidden wrote *good-bye*, and the writing stopped.

"Most of the time I did not know what letter was coming next," Whidden said later, adding that he was aware of what was happening, but couldn't control it. "My hand was numb. I had a feeling of numbness about my heart as well."

Afterwards, Whidden sat as limp as a rag doll and stared into space until he collected the energy to stand weakly. Still dazed, he walked unsteadily as far as the dining room, where he accepted Mary Ellen's invitation to a game of forty-fives. He couldn't concentrate on the cards, though, and soon the tingling sensations returned. He went back to the bedroom and asked Prince to get "It" to leave him. He picked up the pencil and the

spirit again took over his hand, writing *good-bye*. Feeling more in control, Whidden returned to the dining room, but the weird sensations returned, frightening him. Prince again asked the spirit to leave. About five minutes later Whidden felt his usual self. He and Prince tried the experiment four more times before leaving the MacDonald house. Each time Whidden's hand became slightly numb and tingly, but he never again entered the strange state or received spirit messages. Whidden vowed never to reveal the complete contents of the strange manuscript. "The happenings at the MacDonald homestead on March 10 were of such a sacred and personal nature, it would be unwise to give them indiscriminate circulation," he said.

The spirit had given proof that it belonged to a person whom the reporter refused to name; and the fact that he couldn't repeat the experience showed that his subconscious mind didn't invent it, Whidden claimed. "I will, as a result, believe to the hour of my death at least, that the fires in Alexander Macdonald's house and the mysterious unfastening of his cattle were caused by spirits," he stated. *Herald* readers eagerly met Whidden's announcement in the March 14 paper that Prince's report would be published the next day. The investigator's promised daily updates had mostly revisited the fires and discussed the weather, but hadn't answered the main question: Was the farm haunted?

Twice during Prince's seclusion at the farm, a movie company visited Caledonia Mills to record the activity with the latest picture technology, but was turned back each time. Cape Breton reporter Dawn Fraser also couldn't get near the farm, but satisfied his curiosity by questioning various neighbours. Less fortunate scribes went away with empty notebooks, searching for new angles on the story. They telegraphed radio expert Guglielmo Marconi about the theory that radio waves had started the fires, which seemed scientific enough to bear investigation. Could radio waves travelling overhead between stations strike downward to cause fires? "Do not think so," came Marconi's brief reply, and that was that.

Italian inventor Guglielmo Marconi

Guglielmo Marconi established wireless stations in England and Massachusetts, but when a storm damaged them he set up apparatus at St. John's, Newfoundland, to receive the first transatlantic radio message in December 1901. He moved the St. John's station to Glace Bay, Cape Breton, and repeated the transmission in reverse a year later.

About the same time, newspapers reported a similar mystery at Alva, Oklahoma, where blue flames leaped from the air to threaten Ona Smith, twenty-three, who was paralyzed and unable to move. Over several days fire scorched two mattresses, other bedding, a calendar, and clothing, all in front of witnesses. At one point, flames burst from a shawl wrapped around the invalid's shoulders as she sat in her wheelchair. The mystery remained unsolved.

Prince's twenty-nine-page report divided the events at Caledonia Mills into two types, according to a ghost-classification method established in the early 1900s. The first, Type A, or physical, included the interference with the livestock, the missing household and farm items, and the fires. Type B, or psychic, included the noises heard by Whidden and Carroll, the simultaneous contact on their arms, and Whidden's automatic writing. Witnesses had described their experiences and observations in complete honesty, but had interpreted them incorrectly, Prince explained. He assessed Mary Ellen as having a mental age of about six, and concluded that she lit the fires while under the influence of a secondary personality, or possessed by a spirit.

Most of the fires started within the reach of someone five feet tall, Mary Ellen's height, Prince explained. Fires that started in higher places involved pieces of burning cotton, which Mary Ellen tossed into nooks and crannies of the bare wooden walls, Prince deduced. No one saw Mary Ellen lighting the fires because they were too busy putting them out. No fires occurred

twice in the same spot, none started when the home was vacant, and none started in plain view, he noted. A glove, burnt match, and ashes found in a recess over the kitchen door also indicated arson, he said. To ensure she wasn't caught, Mary Ellen started the fires with something like odourless, easily ignited separator oil, which burns on wet paper. If it didn't burn itself out, it would dry the paper enough to burst into flame after the girl moved to another spot, said Prince.

Prince's discovery of bottles of separator oil, kerosene, and turpentine in the kitchen rafters proved that Mary Ellen had access to the chemicals, he said. He deemed the first fire around the kitchen flue to be accidental, but that the excitement had prompted Mary Ellen's second personality to reenact the events in order to get attention from Alex and Janet; most fires started in their presence, and only two in Mary Ellen's sleeping area, he added. Prince claimed that stories about bochdans had inspired the girl to play tricks by hiding household items and loosening the cows.

While Prince judged the fires and mischief as uncontrollable acts by a mentally deficient girl, he deemed Carroll's and Whidden's experiences to be truly paranormal events. Both men had experienced the same slaps and noises on their second night in the house, when their imaginations had settled. Prince ruled out hallucinations, fatigue, hypothermia, pranksters, and the creaks of an old house, which left no other explanation but ghosts. He figured Carroll was influenced by Whidden's psychic abilities, later demonstrated by the reporter's automatic writing.

Whidden wrote two correct pieces of information that he could not possibly have known, proving that a spirit communicated with him, Prince said. That spirit confessed to lighting the fires and loosening the cows, so it must have also possessed Mary Ellen, Prince said. Prince also diagnosed Mary Ellen with a mental illness, a hysteria that prompted her to set the fires, just like he suspected happened to Esther Cox in the Great Amherst Mystery thirty years earlier. Mary Ellen would outgrow

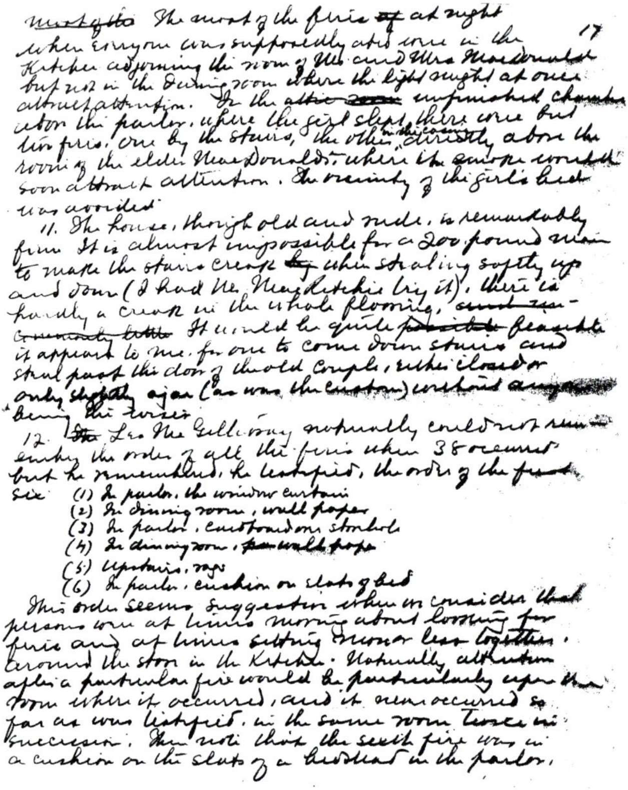

~~most of the~~ The most of the fires ~~of~~ at night 17
when everyone was supposedly abed were in the
Kitchen adjoining the room of Mr and Mrs MacDonald
but not in the Dining room where the light might at once
attract attention. In the ~~attic room~~ unfinished chamber
above the parlor, where the girl slept, there were but
two fires, one by the stairs, the other in the corner directly above the
room of the elder MacDonalds, where the smoke would
soon attract attention. The vicinity of the girl's bed
was avoided.
11. The house, though old and rude, is remarkably
firm. It is almost impossible for a 200 pound man
to make the stairs creak ~~by~~ when stealing softly up
and down (I had Mr. MacRitchie try it). There is
hardly a creak in the whole flooring, ~~and con-~~
~~sequently [illegible]~~ It would be quite ~~possible~~ feasible
it appears to me, for one to come down stairs and
steal past the door of the old couple, either closed or
only slightly ajar (as was the custom) without anyone
being the wiser.
12. ~~Mr~~ Leo McGillivray naturally could not remember
the order of all the fires when 38 occurred
but he remembered, he testified, the order of the first
six (1) In parlor, the window curtain
(2) In dining room, wall paper
(3) In parlor, cupboard over stovehole
(4) In dining room, ~~[illegible]~~ wall paper
(5) Upstairs, rags
(6) In parlor, cushion on slats of bed
This order seems suggestive when we consider that
persons were at times moving about looking for
fires and at times sitting more or less together
around the stove in the kitchen. Naturally attention
after a particular fire would be particularly upon the
room where it occurred, and it never occurred so
far as was testified, in the same room twice in
succession. Then note that the sixth fire was in
a cushion on the slats of a bedstead in the parlor.

A sample of Prince's handwritten conclusion about the Caledonia Mills case, archived at Acadia University in Wolfville, Nova Scotia

the disorder and Whidden would recover from his experience, Prince predicted. He also predicted, correctly, that the people of Caledonia Mills would not accept his findings.

He presented his report to the *Halifax Herald*, vowing that he'd never conduct another newspaper-sponsored investigation again because of the public attention. Newspapers other than

the *Herald* published reports that were incorrectly attributed to Prince and members of his team; and one printed forged interviews with him and with Mary Ellen, putting sentences in the girl's mouth that she "could not have formulated to save her life," Prince said angrily. Prince published his report in the *Journal of the American Society for Psychical Research*, Volume 19, and sent his handwritten copy to the Logan Collection of Canadiana at Acadia University in Wolfville, where his former classmate, Dr. G. B. Cutten, was president. Prince apologized to Dalhousie University in Halifax for neglecting to visit, congratulated Dennis on funding an important investigation, and whirled out of the province on March 17, 1922.

"On the whole, Dr. Prince's report may be termed satisfactory and in accord with the investigations previously made in abnormal psychology," said Dr. Cutten. Current poltergeist research indicated that the mischievous spirits often act in the presence of "a defective girl" who is unaware she caused the activity, he added.

While in New York that spring to participate in séances, Sir Arthur Conan Doyle supported Prince's conclusions. Mary Ellen channeled the ghost of a "naughty boy" who continued his mischief after death, the author told New York reporters in April. The Caledonia Mills mystery was certainly caused by the same type of spiritual possession as the Esther Cox case, Conan Doyle claimed. "Yes, there are malevolent spirits on the other side," he said. "But spirits, malevolent or mischievous, are not allowed to do real harm. The Antigonish house really did not take fire, did it? There's a law on the other side that no spirit may do harm to a mortal. They may alarm people, but that is a good thing; it takes a rough jolt to arouse some people to a realization of things." Easy for Doyle to say from his New York comfort, far from the bleak reality of a family forced from its home in Caledonia Mills.

In preparation for her stage career, Peachie and Maggie Carroll bought Mary Ellen a green gingham gown and arranged for this 1922 studio portrait, autographed by the subject.

CHAPTER 5

THE AFTERMATH

In the absence of strong evidence against Mary Ellen, annoyed at Prince's assessment of her, and suspicious of his methods, the people of Caledonia Mills and Roman Valley concluded that the American investigator had not solved the mystery. They remained convinced that spooks had caused the weird events on the farm. One unidentified man humourously summed up the public confusion in a twelve-verse ballad, and sold copies across North America for a quarter each (see "Ballad of Caledonia Mills," p. 115).

On May 7, 1922, the MacDonalds moved back to the farm to plant their crops. Some minor fires took place, including one that completely destroyed Janet's new window curtains, as witnessed by two visitors. On another occasion, a neighbour saw smoke curling from a basket that, upon investigation, turned out to be four smouldering balls of yarn. On June 7, fire severely damaged the big room upstairs, where Mary Ellen slept and where Janet kept her loom. The flames apparently started in the cushion where Janet sat to weave. After that fire, Alex and Janet abandoned their home forever. They moved to Alder River to live with their daughter, Mary Quirk, and her husband, William, although Alex returned to the property to continue farming. The fires did not follow them. "The spooks are still in Antigonish," commented the *New Glasgow Evening News*. "Will someone please page Dr. Prince?"

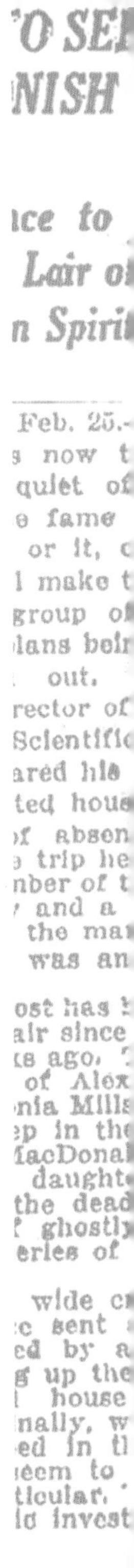
'O SE
NISH
ice to
Lair o
n Spiri
Feb. 25.-
s now t
quiet o
e fame
or it, c
l make t
group o
lans bei
out.
rector o
Scientific
ared his
ted hou
of absen
trip he
nber of t
and a
the ma
was an
ost has
air since
s ago.
of Alex
nia Mills
p in the
lacDonal
daught
the dead
ghostly
eries of
wide c
c sent
ed by a
g up the
house
nally, w
ed in t
eem to
ticular.
id invest

The same day, June 7, Mary Ellen arrived in New Glasgow. Peachie Carroll and his wife, Maggie, met her at the railway station and took her home with them to Pictou. They arranged a speaking tour of large cities in Canada and the United States, where the detective planned to describe the Caledonia Mills mystery while Mary Ellen basked in public attention and proved that she wasn't the halfwit described in Dr. Prince's report. "Mary Ellen would hardly be taken for one with whom the spirits communed," a *New Glasgow Evening News* reporter wrote. "Seen at close range, she is a disappointment." Although the round-faced girl's hazel eyes held a glint of humour, she looked too childishly innocent to have carried out the nefarious actions that had forced her family from their home. However, Dr. Prince was the expert about the unknown, so "we must bow to that decision" the reporter added sarcastically, concluding that, "The movies will provide an attractive field for her psychical powers...She should enjoy the attention."

The Carrolls outfitted Mary Ellen with a new wardrobe, including a green gingham gown that she wore for a studio portrait. She made one stage appearance in Pictou around the first of July, but interest in the case had finally waned so the rest of the tour was cancelled. By the third week of July, Carroll returned to his usual job and Mary Ellen left Pictou. It's unclear if Mary Ellen returned to live with Alex and Janet at that point or whether she visited her birth family in Westville. There was certainly no peace for her in Caledonia Mills.

Hordes of sightseers, amateur ghost-hunters, and curious reporters with their cameras visited the famous spook farm to pose for photos and commune with the spirits. Local residents made extra money guiding tourists to the remote site, risking their clients' fancy vehicles over the gravel road and long lane to the farm. Occasional lineups meant that visitors had to wait for one party to leave before ascending the lane to the farm. It became too much for the MacDonalds, who were still trying to work

The MacDonald farm became popular with tourists, who were guided there by locals. A Duggan, possibly related to Mary Ellen's birth mother, Annie, took this group of Americans to the site about 1930. The windows are still intact in this photo.

the property. Alex finally placed an advertisement in the *Casket*'s July 22 issue, banning sightseers. Bishop James Morrison, of the Roman Catholic Diocese of Antigonish, also took a stand against people gawking at the MacDonald farm. "The things that happened there were not of this earth," one resident quoted him as

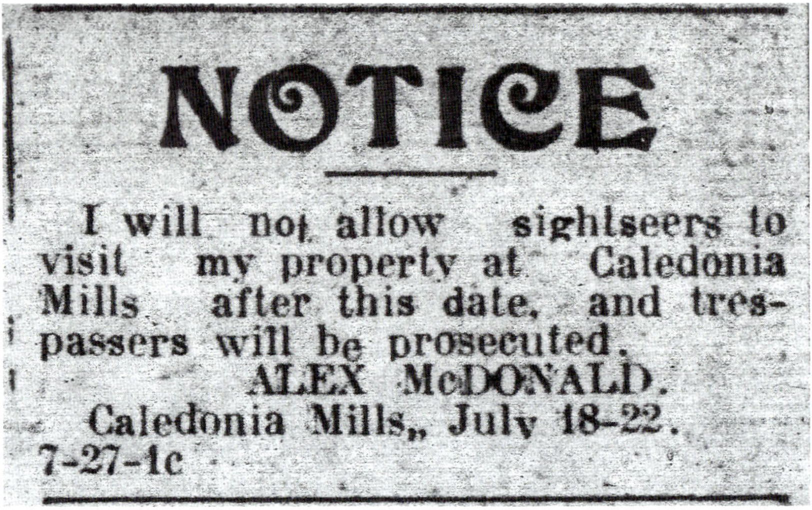
NOTICE

I will not allow sightseers to visit my property at Caledonia Mills after this date, and trespassers will be prosecuted.

ALEX McDONALD.

Caledonia Mills, July 18-22.

7-27-1c

Alex MacDonald's ad in the *Casket* (Antigonish) urging people to stay away from his farm

saying, a statement that likely attracted the curious rather than keeping them away.

The tourists retreated, but Mary Ellen had fewer options—she had to earn a living. So, after her failed stage career, she returned to live briefly with Alex and Janet. Then, like many teenage girls of the era, she found work as a domestic servant with the Bonner family in Antigonish. It seems she didn't stay long in the job, maybe because her life in the town of Antigonish held little happiness. Students thought it great sport to light wooden matches and toss them after her as she walked through town, while they jeered, "Spook! Spook! Mary Ellen Spook!"

In Antigonish some people felt sorry for Mary Ellen, but others thought she got only what she deserved. They believed she was either possessed by evil spirits, or she had deliberately set out to destroy the lives of her adopted parents for her own mysterious purposes. Around Caledonia Mills, resentment festered at

Mary Ellen, Antigonish 'Ghost,' Sent to Asylum for Insane

HALIFAX, N. S., Oct. 12.—Memories of the ghost of Antigonish, for which experts and psychics sought fruitlessly several months ago, were revived today when it became known that Mary Ellen McDonald, the 15-year-old girl whose stories of the phantom were largely instrumental in the systematic search for it, had been admitted to the Nova Scotia Hospital for the Insane here.

Dr. Walter Prince, Director of the American Institute for Scientific Research, after a persistent investigation, decided that Mary Ellen was responsible for the manifestations of a spirit presence which had excited the countryside.

A New York newspaper reported in October 1922 that Mary Ellen had been committed to the Provincial Hospital for the Insane of Nova Scotia.

the outside world for the public scrutiny and ridicule of the MacDonalds; they just wanted to be left alone.

In October 1922, American newspapers reported that Mary Ellen had been admitted several weeks earlier to the Provincial Hospital for the Insane of Nova Scotia at Dartmouth, after being arrested for trying to burn a barn. No such news appeared in Nova Scotia publications, and Alex and Janet refused to speak with outside reporters. Unnamed provincial officials described the couple as angry about Mary Ellen's arrest, which puzzled them because they assumed Alex and Janet would appreciate having the fire threat removed from their lives. Meanwhile, Mary Ellen didn't know why she was incarcerated, and laughed and cried hysterically as she told nurses she'd been arrested for breaking dishes.

Officials quietly moved the girl from Antigonish to the Dartmouth hospital in mid-September, fearful that a public uproar would satisfy Mary Ellen's quest for fame. Hospital superintendent Dr. Fred Lawlor also worried that her presence would upset other inmates. He described Mary Ellen as a common, garden-variety

moron with the mind of an uninteresting four-year-old, albeit one who had attracted international media attention. According to Lawlor, she should have been locked up two years earlier, and would likely spend the rest of her life in the institution. Mary Ellen spent her first weeks at the hospital in solitary confinement, sitting quietly and staring out the window at Halifax Harbour. Lawlor said that he would give her small tasks appropriate to her backward mind, but his immediate treatment would be to leave her alone with absolutely no access to flammable materials.

American newspapers' earlier exaggerated stories about the MacDonald family's plight made the asylum reports suspicious, but they conflicted only slightly with other accounts about Mary Ellen's activities at that time. According to the American papers, Mary Ellen first moved to New Glasgow to be near family members, until she met a man named "Jackson" and went with him to Montreal, where she worked as a waitress. Mary Ellen did leave Nova Scotia, but the actual date of her departure is uncertain. Regardless, she temporarily dropped out of sight after the summer of 1922. (It appears that she was still absent when Alex died on March 26, 1923, at Roman Valley.)

After living with the Quirks, Alex and Janet moved to Roman Valley in December 1922. Alex fell ill with pneumonia and asthma on March 12, 1923, and died two weeks later, just three months after his seventy-second birthday. His obituary in the *Casket* described him as a quiet, patient and "industrious man who always laboured hard to make an honest living, and who was honest and upright in his dealings with others." It mentioned his wife and daughter, and a "stepdaughter to whom he was always a good, kind and faithful father," referring to Mary Ellen. The obituary for Alex's older brother, Donald Allan Dhu, who died a month earlier in Glace Bay, appeared in the same newspaper issue. Following a March 28 funeral mass at St. Patrick's Roman Catholic Church in Guysborough Intervale, Alex was buried in the parish cemetery.

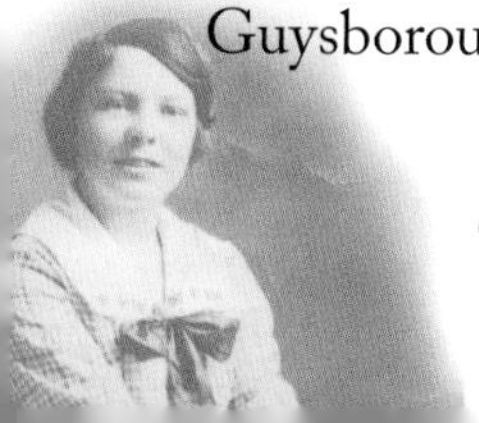

Both Alex and Janet MacDonald were buried in St. Patrick's Roman Catholic churchyard at Guysborough Intervale.

Janet moved in with the Quirks, and lived with them until her death at the age of eighty-one. Some reports claim that she died March 17, 1930, of burns—appropriate for fire-spook stories. However, the Janet MacDonald who died on that date was a widow from St. Andrews who was buried in the parish cemetery there, although there is no grave marker. Janet (Cameron) MacDonald, the daughter of John and Mary Boyd Cameron and widow of Alex MacDonald, died eighteen months after that, on Sept. 12, 1932, of "senility," another way of saying old age.

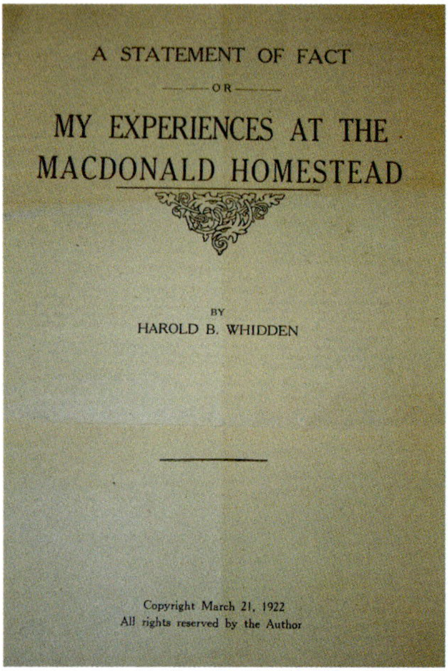

A STATEMENT OF FACT

OR

MY EXPERIENCES AT THE MACDONALD HOMESTEAD

BY

HAROLD B. WHIDDEN

Copyright March 21, 1922

All rights reserved by the Author

Harold Whidden described his paranormal experiences in his self-published pamphlet in March 1921.

She was buried near Alex at the Guysborough Intervale cemetery, although there is no record of either grave. Area residents suspect their burial markers disappeared during a 1960s cemetery cleanup, when broken headstones were carted away and buried at a North Intervale farm. This was before the passing of the 1998 *Nova Scotia Cemeteries and Monuments Protection Act*, which forbids the damaging of gravesites. Uncertain about the location of old, unmarked graves, parishioners opened a new cemetery.

The mystery affected others besides the MacDonalds. Newspaperman Harold Whidden's brush with the supernatural rattled him severely and affected his health, which was already compromised by the gas attack during the First World War. Sensitive to public comment, he published a pamphlet on March 21, 1922, called *A Statement of Fact, or My Experiences at the MacDonald Homestead*. In it, he described the incident as incredible but real, and profoundly disturbing. Something powerful and mysterious had worked through him—and maybe Mary Ellen—Whidden said, warning that no one should experiment lightly with the supernatural.

Whidden then left Nova Scotia for an extended trip to Montreal, Toronto, Ottawa, and Niagara Falls. He stayed with friends of *Herald* artist Donald McRitchie, attended social

functions, and toured the various attractions in an effort to forget the spook farm. His fame preceded him, though, and people everywhere wanted to discuss the mystery. "We have talked very little about the Caledonia Mills affair," he wrote to his family on April 2, 1922. "But on several occasions we simply could not avoid it."

Whidden returned to Antigonish on April 13, declaring himself rested, in good health, and ready to get back to work. While away, several people encouraged him to write a book, and he publicly stated his intention to do so. But the book remained unwritten, maybe because he met his future wife, Clara Cunningham. They became well-liked and prominent members of Antigonish society, happily putting the Caledonia Mills mystery behind them.

Peachie Carroll, who, according to local lore, never lost a case, publicly challenged Prince's conclusions in the March 25 issue of the *Montreal Standard*. Prince had offered no concrete proof that Mary Ellen had started the fires and had incorrectly assessed her intelligence as that of a six-year-old, the detective said. "For the chances she has had, she is real bright," said Carroll. "If Dr. Prince has discovered the solution to the mystery, why doesn't he claim the reward?" The Caledonia Mills mystery was Carroll's last big case, which he described in the *Pictou Advocate* in 1922 and again in his 1923 memoirs, *Life and Adventures of Detective Peter Owen Carroll*, along with scathing comments on Prince's investigation. He went to his grave believing in Mary Ellen's innocence.

As for Mary Ellen, she showed up in Halifax in the spring of 1926, after her apparent release from a three-and-a-half-year stint in the Provincial Hospital for the Insane of Nova Scotia. She found a job washing dishes at the Frisco Café, a Chinese restaurant on Sackville Street, near Water Street, and boarded with the Fenerty family, who lived a couple of blocks up the hill on Argyle Street. With no friends in the city and even less of an

DR. PRINCE'S VERSION OF FIRES CHALLENGED BY DETECTIVE.

Peter O. Carroll Says Prince Has Failed To Prove That Girl Set Fires. Peachie's Story of the "Spook's" Visit When Wrist Was Slapped.

Detective Carroll challenged Dr. Prince's conclusions in an article he wrote for the *Montreal Standard*, which also appeared in the *Pictou Advocate*.

inclination to share her personal story, Mary Ellen gravitated towards other displaced and disadvantaged people, including her Asian workmates. Many Chinese brought an opium tradition to Canada and favoured the substance over the Nova Scotia drug of choice, alcohol. Forms of opium were used at this time to medicate asylum inmates, so Mary Ellen may have developed a dependency on the drug at the insane asylum. Whatever the case, her association with Chinese businesses, ex-convicts, and assorted suspicious characters along the Halifax waterfront brought her to the attention of city police.

On Sunday morning, March 13, 1927, a year after cops on the downtown beat first noticed her presence, Officer Yeadon arrested Mary Ellen while she lay in bed, partially dressed, with a Chinese laundry worker. At her March 19 appearance in magistrate's court, Officers Kelloch and Virtue described Mary Ellen as a healthy-looking twenty-one-year-old woman who had been hanging around Chinese cafés and laundries. She was the same person involved in the Antigonish spook incident a few years earlier, they testified.

Mary Ellen testified that she felt sick the day she was arrested, so she had left her rooming house for Bevis' grocery store on Upper Water Street to get something for her tummy. Two men met her along the way and gave her alcohol, which immediately made her sick. Believing the liquor was doped, she asked for a drink of water at a Chinese laundry. The owner, whom she had never met before, gave her water and suggested she lie down until she felt better. She fell asleep and didn't remember anything else until she woke up with the officer standing over her.

The magistrate found her guilty of vagrancy, also known as night walking, a term that meant prostitution. During her sentencing hearing, her defence lawyer said the spook-case publicity had gone to Mary Ellen's head and affected her morals, causing her downfall. The magistrate sentenced her to six months in Halifax city prison. "That's easy," Mary Ellen remarked to her jailers as they led her away. Indeed, after almost four years in the Provincial Hospital, six months in the city jail was a piece of cake.

Prisoner Number 135, Mary Ellen MacDonald, was released on September 18, 1927, at ten o'clock in the morning. Although she kept in touch with old friends from Caledonia Mills, Mary Ellen's exact activities after 1927 remain unclear. It's possible she worked in Montreal, as the city directory listed a Miss M. E. MacDonald, clerk, in the early 1930s. Maybe that's where she went with the man named Jackson.

Eventually Mary Ellen, without Jackson but with hordes of other eastern Canadians, migrated to the northern Ontario nickel town of Sudbury, where jobs were plentiful. She settled on Borgia Street, once known as the toughest street in Canada and responsible for Sudbury's high crime rate. On pay day, miners flocked to the short street's illicit gambling and bawdy houses, where prostitutes lured clients into rooms so that their male conspirators could rob them, and where murder was the easiest answer to most problems. Borgia Street served as an initiation for rookie cops, who were sometimes stripped of their weapons

Mary Ellen moved to Sudbury's Borgia Street, a neighbourhood infamous for crime. Like the MacDonald spook house it no longer exists.

and clothing by the street's inhabitants before being sent on their way. Police dealt with prostitutes by ordering them out of town within twenty-four hours, with the threat of jail time. Mary Ellen stayed out of jail and in the city, so either she wasn't plying the trade, or she never got caught.

By the early 1960s, she had changed her name to Ella and then to Helen McGuire, and ran a small shop and boarding house at 30 Borgia Street, at the corner of Lisgar Street, a neighbourhood of older-style homes that offered rented rooms to transients

Mary Ellen, by then known as Helen McGuire, appears happy and healthy in this 1970s photo of her taken at her Sudbury home. A priest was supposed to be in this photo with her, but when it was developed, he'd disappeared.

and newcomers. Transplanted Nova Scotians told people back home that Mary Ellen's business served as a front for prostitution and bootlegging under the colourful nickname, "Bucket of Blood." She eventually married Austin Edward "Red" McGuire, a Coca Cola plant worker from Coburg, Ontario, who was once a boarder at her place. They had a daughter, Theresa, whose date and place of birth is unclear, but she must have been born in the 1950s because, as it turned out, she was old enough to have had four children by 1977.

When the city bulldozed the neighbourhood about 1970 for an urban renewal project, the McGuires moved to 179 Shaughnessy Street at the edge of downtown Sudbury, taking their lodgers with them. Six years later, on February 24, 1977, Austin died, at seventy-three. His obituary listed his survivors as his wife, Helen; his daughter, Theresa, who lived in Vancouver with her four children; and two sisters. Mary Ellen stayed at 179 Shaughnessy, augmenting her small pension and paying for upkeep and repairs by renting rooms to four lodgers, while a fifth did odd jobs in return for a room. Confined to a wheelchair, and with her eyesight failing, Mary Ellen shared her ground-floor apartment with a roommate and her eight-year-old cocker spaniel, Queenie.

Mary Ellen's world crashed again in 1981 when the landlord evicted her and her tenants and demolished the house to make room for trendy restaurants, a theatre, and, interestingly, given Mary Ellen's history, a fire station. (In 2012 only a soup kitchen and a homeless shelter signified the neighbourhood's humble beginnings.) "I don't like moving," Mary Ellen told *Northern Life* reporter Brian Inkster, who wrote a 1981 story about her housing problem. She didn't tell Inkster that tragedy first uprooted her as a child of four, or that mysterious circumstances forced her from her next home at fifteen. The Provincial Hospital was home for four years, but a prison sentence had interrupted her new start in downtown Halifax. Rough Borgia Street had been her first home since Caledonia Mills, and her first as an independent adult. Although she hadn't experienced any fires for fifty-nine years, Mary Ellen was now uprooted again. This time she could have moved to a nursing home, but she hated institutions and didn't want to give up Queenie or her lodgers of seventeen years. "My dog comes with me. She's a very nice dog. I don't want a low rental. I want a home. I want to take my roomers with me, where I could make my own living. I like to pay my own way," she told Inkster, who later described her as helpless but determined. "I'm independent, all by myself," she claimed.

But Mary Ellen couldn't stop progress. She moved to her final home at 1231 Northway Avenue in Sudbury, where she

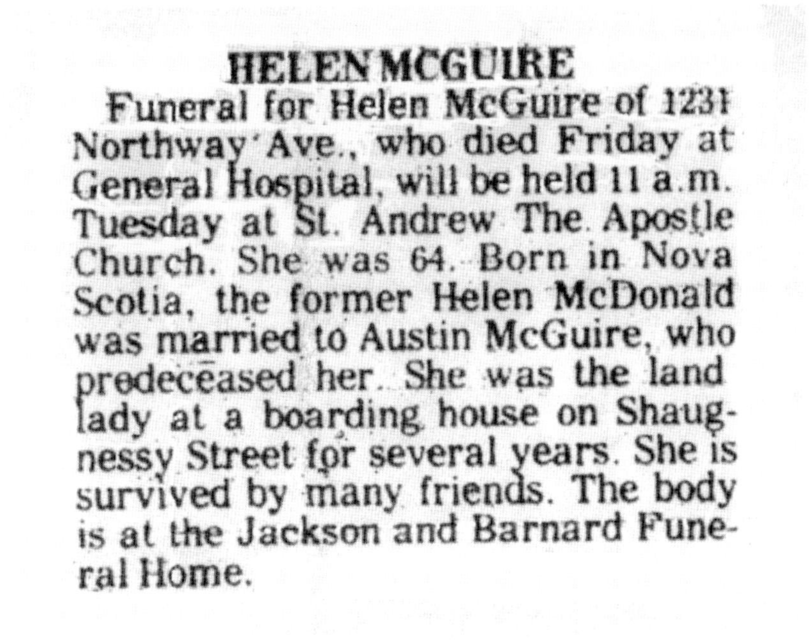

HELEN MCGUIRE
Funeral for Helen McGuire of 1231 Northway Ave., who died Friday at General Hospital, will be held 11 a.m. Tuesday at St. Andrew The Apostle Church. She was 64. Born in Nova Scotia, the former Helen McDonald was married to Austin McGuire, who predeceased her. She was the land lady at a boarding house on Shaugnessy Street for several years. She is survived by many friends. The body is at the Jackson and Barnard Funeral Home.

The obituary for Mary Ellen MacDonald (Helen McGuire), as it appeared in the *Sudbury Star* on June 8, 1987

stayed until her death in the local hospital six years later. Like her previous abodes at Caledonia Mills, Borgia Street, and Shaughnessy Street, this address was also erased from the landscape. Part of Northway Avenue, a short street of comfortable bungalows and a church, remains, but 1231 is now part of a modern subdivision of multi-family dwellings.

Mary Ellen's obituary appeared in the *Sudbury Star* on June 8, 1987, with no mention of any children or siblings. Mary Ellen's brother Walter lived until 1995, when he was ninety; her brother John had drowned earlier in Hamilton, Ontario; and, as of the 1960s, her sister, Anne, lived in Lethbridge, Alberta. The obituary listed Mary Ellen's age as sixty-four but she was actually eighty, given her birthdate of August 21, 1906. However, her

death *did* occur about sixty-four years after Alex's death and the sixty-fourth anniversary of her departure from Caledonia Mills; she might have started counting her new life from that date.

Mary Ellen's death did not solve the Caledonia Mills puzzle, nor did it end the strange events at the farm. Although the spirit promised, through Whidden, to leave the farm alone, people began reporting their own eerie experiences in the area as soon as the reporter's first accounts were published in 1922. Some were real, but others were manufactured or embellished. N. Carroll MacIntyre, author of *The Fire-Spook of Caledonia Mills*, was confronted with the mystery in the form of a strange, white horse as he passed the vacant MacDonald homestead late one night in the early 1960s. He never found the owner. When a guide showed him the farm in 1961, MacIntyre took a piece of charred shingle as a souvenir of the ruined house. Removing anything from the farm was said to bring bad luck, but he thought no one would notice. However, MacIntyre suggested that his guide knew, psychically. Before leaving the property, he persuaded MacIntyre to restore the wood sliver and, ultimately, avoid the farm's curse.

The next time MacIntyre explored the farm, there was no guide, so he took a hand-painted egg cup that he found near the foundation, maybe one of those that had crashed to the floor so many years earlier. He placed the egg cup at his family's cottage, which burned soon afterwards, proving the jinx to MacIntyre. When he tried to fly to Sudbury to interview Mary Ellen, the aircraft engine died unaccountably, forcing the plane to make an emergency landing. In 2011 he warned of the dangers of becoming too involved in the mystery.

The family that moved into the house rented by the MacDonalds after the January 8, 1922, fires reported that a particular kitchen cupboard often caught fire. Chairs moved on their own and knocks would come on the door—with no one outside. The mail delivery man and other people travelling past the MacDonald farm frequently reported more white horses

Carroll MacIntyre, the author of the 1985 book *The Fire Spook of Caledonia Mills*, became part of the legend when he had his own strange experiences at the MacDonald farm.

and black dogs, including one canine trotting along the fence's narrow top rail. Chilling, white fog suddenly enveloped passersby, and car engines died for no apparent reason. In the early 1970s a seminary student took a brick from the site to show his peers back in New York. When he stored it temporarily in his aunt's shed in Antigonish County, the shed caught fire that very night. Also in the 1970s, a group of St. Francis Xavier University students parked their Ford Mercury near the road and walked to the farm. Upon their return, they found the car burned beyond recognition, except for the letters "ME" in the word "Mercury," Mary Ellen's initials. In 2012, a trucker vowed never to return after his vehicle mysteriously broke down after a trip to the farm, an event he blamed on the spook.

Events that could happen anywhere became mysterious if they were connected to the spook farm, but some experiences were arranged to frighten people. Among the pranksters was a man who, in 2011, admitted to organizing fires at the farm in the 1980s for university students' initiation. Even Peachie Carroll, a practiced prankster, allowed friends to believe the tall tales, and occasionally embellished them. But not all the stories were jokes. Older residents still recall their parents and grandparents

A visitor searching for the fire spook perched in the home's open window for this 1930 photo.

seriously discussing strange blue-and-orange fires at the homestead, occurring outside the documented events of January 1922, and unreported by Whidden or anyone else.

While many people blamed Mary Ellen for the fires, MacIntyre accused Janet in his 1985 book. He based his suspicions

on Harold Whidden's automatic writing, which had been stored at the Roman Catholic glebe house in St. Andrews, and then turned over to Bishop Morrison, who burned them. Several people saw the pages—including the parish priests, Alex's brother Dan, Walter Prince, Alex, and Janet—and someone told MacIntyre that Mary Boyd Cameron's spirit had guided Whidden's writing. Through him, she confessed that she had started the fires and loosed the cows because Janet had smothered her twenty-two years earlier. No one talked openly about any involvement by Janet until the 1980s, which is why Mary Ellen had borne most of the responsibility.

According to local lore, Janet told her side of the story to Duncan Borrodale MacDonald and his brother in the United States, who helped Janet financially after Alex's death. She swore both men to secrecy during her lifetime, but even after her death they would never divulge any information. Duncan died just before an appointment with a writer to confirm some fairly simple details about the Caledonia Mills story. In a different time and place, his brother began telling the story, but was interrupted by an emergency call to work, where he was an electrical linesman. He was killed on the job; an eerie coincidence that only added to the spook theories.

Backing up the case against Janet were the people who swore they had encountered her ghost. One particular man, whom Janet disliked and had ordered off the farm, ventured onto the property after her death, only to be attacked by the spirit of "the Old One," as Janet was called. If it hadn't been for his dogs defending him by growling and biting the attacker, he'd be dead, he told friends. He spent two weeks in bed recovering from the experience, a fact witnessed by neighbours. Another man, who squatted in vacant farmhouses around the countryside, told people he'd fired his gun at Janet's ghost as it stood in a corner of the derelict MacDonald home. "Something queer was going on up there," one self-described skeptic said, before

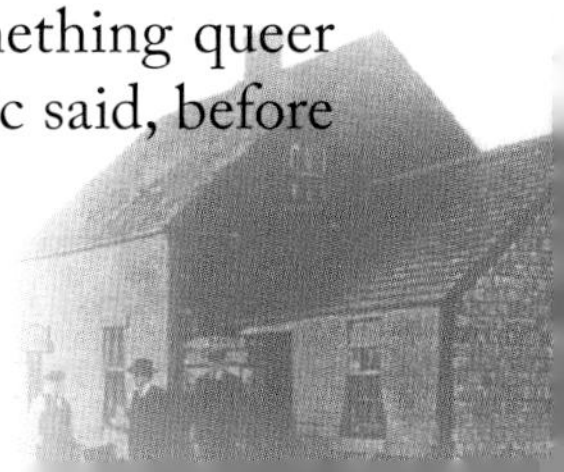

Mary (MacDonald) Quirk

Mary MacDonald was twenty-nine when she married farmer William Leo Quirk, thirty-two, on October 10, 1916, at St. Andrew's Roman Catholic Church in St. Andrews, a ceremony witnessed by Alfred Quirk and Gertie Kelly. William, son of John and Jane (MacDonald) Quirk, took his bride back to his home in Alder River, Guysborough County. In 1929 the couple adopted a two-year-old girl from the Little Flower Orphanage at Bras d'Or, Cape Breton. Little Mary Estelle died six weeks later of pneumonia. Mary and William raised two other children, a boy and a girl. Their son went to Ontario as a young man, and their daughter was still living in Antigonish as of 2012. William Quirk died of stomach cancer in 1947. Mary moved to Salmon River Lake to board with a MacDonald family, where she died in June 1960.

recounting the hair-raising story about the Old One's attack on the local resident. He ended with the emphasis, "That's true, too." Others believe that Andrew MacDonald's spirit began haunting the family in 1910, the same year he died and Mary Ellen moved in, taking his revenge slowly until the family was forced out, just as he had vowed on that stormy November night in 1903.

According to area residents, either Andrew, or Janet, or Mary Boyd Cameron, or all three continue to haunt the place to the present day. It's unclear whether the various priests who prayed at the farm over the years were official exorcists, but they didn't close the case or ease people's fears. Even speaking about the experiences ninety years later caused anxiety around Caledonia Mills, based on concerns that the spook would return or that outsiders would mock them. Mary MacDonald Quirk, described as a pleasant, quiet woman who attended mass regularly at Guysborough Intervale, sternly refused to discuss the affair throughout her life. Her family members and neighbours around Alder River followed suit. In more recent years, those willing

to discuss the spook farm anonymously had no personal fears concerning ghosts, but they didn't poke fun, either.

"Maybe it was all a misunderstanding," said a young woman, who noted that older, more religious people seemed caught up in the spook stories. The younger generation doesn't go to church and doesn't believe in ghosts, except for enjoying some Halloween thrills around the MacDonald farm. Today, much more is known about mental illness, so if Mary Ellen did set the fires she might be treated more kindly, she said.

A grainy photo of Mary Ellen (left), Alex (centre), and Janet (right), shows none of their features except their comparative height. Mary Ellen was almost as tall as Alex, but Janet's height is hard to determine because she is standing on a different level.

CHAPTER 6

THE MYSTERY CONTINUES

What really happened?

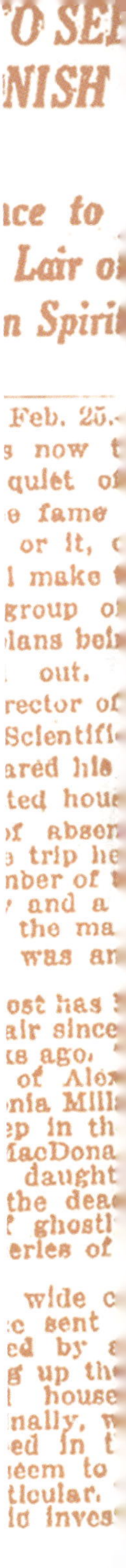

More than ninety years after the MacDonalds moved out, it's unlikely the mystery can be solved. All eyewitnesses have died, and the stories about the MacDonalds' fire spook have been embellished through almost a century of repetition, translation from Gaelic to English and back, and confusion about the original facts of the case.

As an example of confused details, Alex MacIsaac, who heard the story from eyewitnesses the day the MacDonalds moved out, told Whidden that a cushion found burning downstairs in the corner of the parlour had been taken upstairs a few days earlier to keep it away from the dog. Eyewitness Leo MacGillivray told Whidden that the burning cushion sat among the slats of the parlour bed. An exaggerated 1922 newspaper article reported that the cushion caught fire upstairs on January 11, while another account from the 1970s quotes a Caledonia Mills resident as having witnessed a cushion igniting while Janet sat on it upstairs.

The sensationalist newspaper story was probably incorrect, as it contained other, more obvious mistakes. MacIsaac's and MacGillivray's accounts are likely true, with the small discrepancy potentially explained if the bed had occupied a corner of the parlour. The story about the cushion burning while Janet sat on it may also be true, and is included here as one of the fires that occurred at the farm in May and June 1922, before the

The MacDonald house and barn still stood in the 1930s, although the years showed. The windows were initially boarded over, but curious sightseers removed the covers along with the window panes and frames. In this image, both chimneys have also been removed.

MacDonalds left for good. Alex stated that the January fires and the escaping cows in 1921 were the farm's only odd events, so any other fires likely happened after Prince's investigation. Others reported independent accounts of their parents and grandparents witnessing fires at the homestead that were also not included in Whidden's documentation.

In another example of inconsistency, witnesses said they extinguished thirty-eight fires on the night of January 11/12, but the individual fires, as well as their sequence, were not accurately documented. An uncounted number of fires started in the wallpaper, but a bed fire wasn't mentioned until Carroll asked about scorch marks among the blankets. Alex told the MacGillivrays he put out six fires while Janet and Mary Ellen went for help, but later told Whidden that at least two fires started in their absence. However, it's possible that he finished extinguishing four that ignited before they left, plus another two afterwards, and that

the evening's confusion contributed to his inability to remember the exact sequence of events.

Whidden recorded no statement that Janet burned her hands while battling the fires while the others remained uninjured; a story that gained significance years later as people pieced together the mystery. As well, accounts about events that supposedly happened before 1922 were not reported until after the fires. These included Mary Boyd Cameron's suspicious death and Andrew's curse, black dogs and disappearing horses, smashed egg cups, missing household items, strange lights and noises around the property, and even the loosed cows. The family confirmed only the cow story in 1922, and some of the other information may have been leaked from Whidden's automatic writing. Several incidents were likely considered normal until the fires made everything spooky; some were probably manufactured after the fact; and others may have been kept secret out of shame or embarrassment.

Whidden's initial reports are the most reliable accounts of the January fires, even allowing for discrepancies between them, the confusion of witnesses, and his occasional flowery prose. He visited the site and carefully recorded the information while people's memories were fresh, noting that he strived for accuracy because the events were so weird. Moreover, Leo MacGillivray later credited the *Herald* reports as accurate.

Both Carroll's and Prince's later accounts and conclusions rely on Whidden's early reports, and are then influenced by each investigator's personal ideas.

Richard S. Lambert, who investigated many paranormal events in Canada for a 1955 book, criticized Prince for his unscientific methods, which, he believed, had resulted in a report biased toward Prince's pet theories. If Prince had been on the scene during the fires or when the cows were loosened, he might have concluded differently, Lambert claimed.

Prince chose to ignore or disdain Alex's statement that fires took place during Mary Ellen and Janet's absence; the five other

By the time this unknown man posed for a 1950s photo beside the MacDonald farmhouse, most of the windows were missing and the interior was gutted. The building collapsed in the 1960s.

witnesses who said it was impossible for her to have lit the fires without being seen, including one who watched her specifically; and the fires in the kitchen ceiling and on the floor that broke out in full view of others. However, he accepted Janet's statement about the teenager's frequent daydreaming as evidence of a psychic disturbance, possibly because it supported his belief that the Caledonia Mills case mimicked the Great Amherst Mystery.

If Mary Ellen attracted a poltergeist, whether the mischievous ghost of Andrew, Mary Boyd Cameron, Janet, or someone else, it didn't act like other cases in which spirits shoved furniture and threw dangerous objects. If a poltergeist caused the fires, why did it need cotton or separator oil to kindle them? Alternatively, if Mary Ellen intentionally set the fires, what was the motive? Prince claimed that Mary Ellen had schemed to get attention from Alex and Janet, indicating he considered her smart enough to plan and carry out complicated tasks without being seen, which

Fire-setting Behaviour

Modern psychology claims that fire-setting behaviour occurs mostly in children of abusive or alcoholic parents, and affects more boys than girls. But girls who set fires may start later in their teens than boys, and tend to do it for entertainment rather than malice. As well, teenaged adopted girls may become sexually promiscuous, act out, or disagree violently when opposed. However, the ample gossip about the MacDonalds gave no hint of abuse, addiction, or any scandalous behaviour except for a single unverified report that Mary Ellen became pregnant as a teenager. Mary Ellen's 1927 conviction indicates that she worked as a prostitute, but as an adult. Even then it's unclear if she worked as a prostitute for money, or if she was a sexual assault victim who was convicted of prostitution according to the era's practices. If Mary Ellen did set fires, it was her only obvious challenging behaviour as a teenager.

contradicted his previous assessment that she had the intellect of a six-year-old. Prince may have been wrong!

Prince's evidence included Mary Ellen's age of fifteen, which would have made her vulnerable to psychic influence and mental illness; and her height of five feet (one-and-a-half metres), which he matched to the height of the fires in the walls. Mary Ellen was actually eight centimetres taller, and full-length photos of the time show she was just slighter shorter than both Alex and Janet. No one saw them set fires either and, just like Mary Ellen, neither was present for every fire.

Prince's discovery of the burned match and glove over the kitchen door and the flammable liquids in the loft pointed to arson. He didn't explain why he found them two months after the fires, while Carroll, Whidden, the MacGillivrays, and others found no accelerants when they searched the house weeks earlier for moonshine, lamp oil, rubbing alcohol, and organic materials that might spontaneously combust. Did Carroll, an extremely tall man and a seasoned detective, miss those obvious clues, or were they placed there later?

Whidden, Carroll, Prince and the artists who accompanied him, Antigonish Police Chief MacLean, and everyone who was asked all agreed that the MacDonalds and their neighbours were upstanding citizens with no idea how the fires started. Even though Prince blamed Mary Ellen, he said she couldn't help herself. As Whidden put it, "If Dr. Prince's theory is correct, that one member of the family in an abnormal psychic state, was used as an instrument to set the fires, then she, in my opinion, was no more responsible for these acts than was I while under the strange influence for over two hours."

Maybe Carroll was right. Maybe no human hands set the fires—and maybe no ghost either. If, as *Herald* readers suggested, a form of phosphorous started the fires, it might have come from a phosphine mixture used to kill farm pests. Alex was illiterate and could not read directions, so he may have decided that if a bit of the phosphine powder worked, more would work better. The substance would have permeated his clothes, the couch and rocker where he sat, the bed where he slept, the paper he handled, and the walls upon which he leaned.

Rodents may have carried the substance into the house on bits of cotton they used as bedding. Once in contact with the damp January air, the phosphine would have turned into a gas that would have ignited to form strangely cool, but bright, flames, and a dense smoke. Throwing water on the burning walls and furniture would have created more gas and more flames. Except for the strange blue lights seen during the previous winter, there is no evidence of fires in the barn, which was likely better ventilated than the house.

Inhaling phosphine causes respiratory illness, a problem that severely affected Janet at the time of the fires and for a while afterwards. She appeared to recover after they moved out of the farmhouse, but Alex continued to visit the place daily. He and Whidden, who had already sustained poisonous gas injuries during the First World War, both developed sore throats and coughs

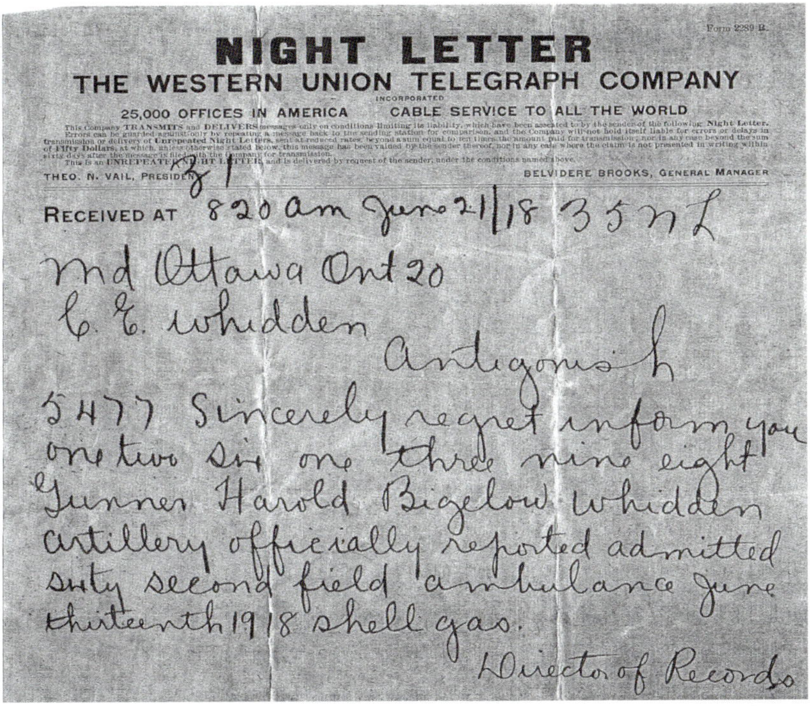

Form 2289 B.

NIGHT LETTER

THE WESTERN UNION TELEGRAPH COMPANY

INCORPORATED

25,000 OFFICES IN AMERICA CABLE SERVICE TO ALL THE WORLD

This Company TRANSMITS and DELIVERS messages only on conditions limiting its liability, which have been assented to by the sender of the following Night Letter. Errors can be guarded against only by repeating a message back to the sending station for comparison, and the Company will not hold itself liable for errors or delays in transmission or delivery of Unrepeated Night Letters, sent at reduced rates, beyond a sum equal to ten times the amount paid for transmission; nor in any case beyond the sum of Fifty Dollars, at which, unless otherwise stated below, this message has been valued by the sender thereof, nor in any case where the claim is not presented in writing within sixty days after the message is filed with the Company for transmission.
This is an UNREPEATED NIGHT LETTER, and is delivered by request of the sender, under the conditions named above.

THEO. N. VAIL, PRESIDENT 2 / BELVIDERE BROOKS, GENERAL MANAGER

RECEIVED AT 820 am June 21/18 35 NL

Md Ottawa Ont 20

C. E. Whidden

Antigonish

5477 Sincerely regret inform you one two six one three nine eight Gunner Harold Bigelow Whidden artillery officially reported admitted sixty second field ambulance June thirteenth 1918 shell gas.

Director of Records

A telegram from the war office to Whidden's parents informed them he'd been injured in a gas attack.

after sleeping on the hay in the farmhouse during Carroll's investigation. Alex's death was caused by pneumonia and asthma.

Methane rising from the soil, as some people suggested, could have ignited to cause fireballs or strange lights, like will-o'-the-wisp, which can intensify phosphine flames. Such lights have been linked to small earthquakes, which might also explain the strange noises reported at the farm. So natural phenomena and the uninformed use of dangerous chemicals might have caused the fires, lights, noises, and Alex's fatal illness; but they don't explain how the cattle got loose, whose arm waved a cloth at the parlour window, what contacted Whidden and Carroll in the

Methane and Phosphine

The legendary big black dog said to haunt the MacDonald farm may have been Alex's dog, Chief, shown here sitting between him (right) and Mary Ellen (left).

Methane, the main component of natural gas, is an explosive, colorless, odourless gas of carbon and hydrogen that develops naturally from rotting organic matter. It is found in swamps, sewers, and coal mines, and its release can cause fires and the appearance of strange lights.

Phosphine is a combination of phosphorous and hydrogen. It is a colourless, poisonous gas that spontaneously ignites in the presence of air to create a dense, white, poisonous smoke, sometimes leaving a white, cottony residue. Depending on additives, powdered forms can become gaseous when wet, and ignite. Both emissions and the powder irritate the human respiratory system. Chronic or intense exposure leads to failure of the lungs, heart, and liver, causing death.

Known since the early 1800s, phosphine and phosphorous, which glows in the dark, were used as emergency flares at sea. Since the early 1900s, farmers have used phosphine to kill rodents and insects, although it was not documented for agricultural use until the 1930s. It is still used against farm pests, with an additive to prevent fires and warnings for safe usage.

middle of that frosty February night or made Whidden scribble pages and pages of pencilled notes, why the MacDonalds' possessions disappeared in the years before 1922, or whose horses and black dogs hung around the farm.

Prince said Mary Ellen's alter ego let the cows loose as a prank, while Carroll concluded that no flesh-and-blood person could have done it. Incidents of braiding the horse's mane and the heifers' tails, and fastening the horse into the cow's stanchion, were reported initially by Whidden, who heard the stories in Antigonish. He believed them until Alex corrected the impression, and it was never repeated in the *Herald*. The only documented interference with the animals happened to the dairy cows, and in only one barn. If it was not ghosts, then it's possible that someone watched Alex from a hiding place within the barn, and began unfastening the nails, ropes, wires, and chains as soon as his back was turned.Alex would have figured it out the first day if it had been Mary Ellen, but he never blamed her. He said the cows escaped while he was absent for no more than three minutes, meaning he had to move fairly quickly from the barn to the house and back, while carrying milk pails over the mud and ice that characterize a Nova Scotia farmyard in March. He probably gave the prankster at least five minutes, enough time to unfasten four stanchions. After Alex moved two cows, the culprit had only two cows to free, so the wires and chains presented less of a challenge than Alex had hoped, especially if he believed he had the problem licked and didn't inspect them immediately.

In similar mischief cases in his career, Carroll usually gave a culprit a quiet, menacing warning to leave the community until the fuss died down. Leo MacGillivray's comment in his March 4 letter that Duncan Borrodale MacDonald went away might indicate that Carroll had a private word with him. Duncan later returned to Caledonia Mills, where local lore says the 1922 events affected him deeply for the rest of his life.

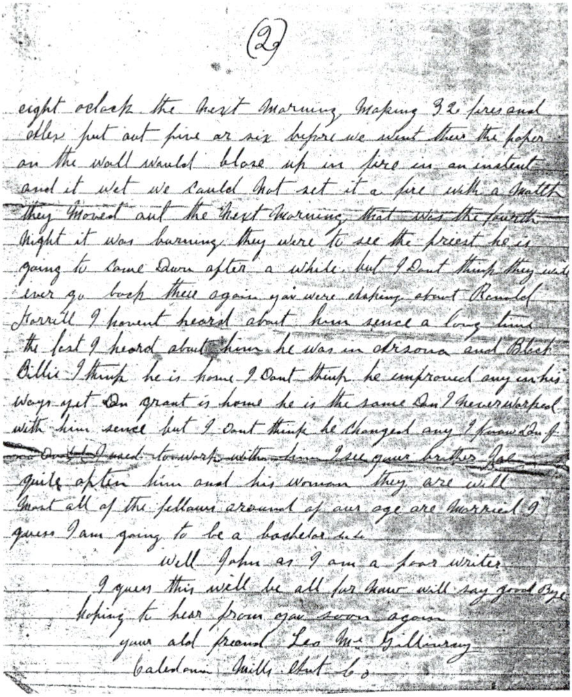

(2)

eight oclock the next morning making 32 fires and
Alex put out five or six before we went there the paper
on the wall would blase up in fire in an instent
and it wet we could not set it a fire with a match
they moved out the next morning that was the fourth
night it was burning they were to see the priest he is
going to come down after a while but I dont think they will
ever go back there again you were asking about Ronald
Farrell I havent heard about him sence a long time
the last I heard about him he was in Arizona and Black
Billie I think he is home I dont think he improved any in his
ways yet Dan grant is home he is the same Dan I never worked
with him sence but I dont think he changed any I know Dan J.
Dan I used to work with him I see your brother Joe
quite aften him and his woman they are well
most all of the fellows around of our age are married I
guess I am going to be a bachelor

Well John as I am a poor writer
I guess this will be all for now will say good Bye
hoping to hear from you soon again
your old friend Leo McGillivray
Caledonia Mills Ant Co.

From Leo MacGillivray's March 4, 1922, letter to John William MacDonald, a former resident of Glencoe near Caledonia Mills, mistakes and all:

> Well John they have been a good many changes around here since you were around. A lot of the people died since. It is getting to be a dull place. The Spook drove Alex MacDonald out and Duncan went away. I suppose you seen the Halifax Herald and all that was in it about the spooks. The statements we made to the reporter was printed as we told them and it was true. It was the queerest thing I ever seen. I never believed much on ghosts but I have to now for I know that no living one could set the fires the night we were there. We got there about half-past nine and between then and five o'clock we put out 31 different fires and one about eight o'clock the next morning making 32 fires and Alex put out five or six before we went there. The paper on the wall would blase up in fire in an instant and it wet. We could not set it a fire with a match. They moved out the next morning. That was the fourth night it was burning. They were to see the priest. He is going to come down after a while, but I don't think they will ever go back there again.

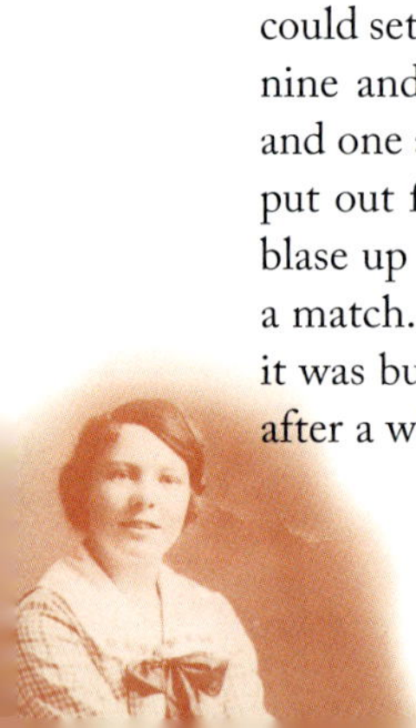

A young schoolteacher who boarded at Duncan Borrodale MacDonald's home in the 1950s told his family how his host kept him up late at night, feeding him homemade biscuits and scaring him with stories of "the Mary Ellen spook farm." Duncan, who acted out the various roles of those involved, had a photo of Mary Ellen. When the photo was taken, a priest had been standing next to her, Duncan told the terrified teacher—there was no priest in the photo. However, until his death in 1974, Duncan was never implicated in the MacDonald farm mystery. It is still conceivable that Carroll and the MacDonalds agreed to keep quiet about some neighbour's part in the affair, passing off the escaped cows as a minor supernatural event compared to the fires. If so, Carroll and Whidden likely hoped that their public challenge would prevent further investigation, and that the public would move on to the next big story. Once Prince got involved, though, it was impossible to admit to a cover-up, especially after Whidden's automatic writing blamed a spirit for letting the cows loose.

Whidden's spirit messages from Mary Boyd Cameron could have been symptoms of post-traumatic stress disorder, which was referred to as "shell shock" at the time, related to the reporter's battle experience in France. Because this condition was attributed to cowardice at the time, few soldiers admitted to emotional or psychological difficulties. Now, it's a recognized injury stemming from war or other violence, with onset sometimes delayed for months or years. Whidden's weeks of immersion in the Caledonia Mills mystery may have triggered an attack. As well, the bloodbath of the war of 1914–18 prompted a search for new spiritual outlets, so communicating with the dead became an accepted trend.

Psychologists and paranormal investigators today view automatic writing as either fraud or a product of the writer's subconscious mind, and not the result of spiritual possession. Whidden seemed too honest and earnest to deliberately aim to fool Prince,

A raised stony area covered in grass and weeds is all that remained of Alex's barn in 2012. Local people say that it took an exceptionally long time for natural bush to regenerate at the farm. The current property owners work hard at maintaining the site's privacy, even though the farm is well off the beaten track—with no signposts or easily-seen landmarks—so it is difficult to find without a guide.

but if he and Carroll had colluded to protect the MacDonalds and their neighbours, he may have subconsciously tried to redirect Prince's attentions away from Mary Ellen and her family. Whidden said he had no prior knowledge of some of the information, but he may simply not have remembered learning it. Regardless, after his tour of Quebec and Ontario in the spring of 1922, it appears that Whidden recovered, gave the mysterious papers to the priest at St. Andrews, and got on with his life. The world will never know for sure what his strange writing said because, after receiving the pages from the priest at St. Andrew's, Bishop James Morrison either destroyed them or hid them very well; as of 2012 they were not among Antigonish diocesan archives, at St. Andrew's, in St. Francis Xavier University archives, or at the Antigonish Heritage Museum.

Neither Prince nor Carroll explained the arm waving through the window. It could have been Mary Ellen or Janet, shaking dust from a rag used to wipe articles clean before packing them for moving, a common housekeeping practice. Witnesses Michael MacGillivray and John Kenny asked only Duncan MacDonald about the whereabouts of the home's occupants. They didn't mention the incident to Janet or Mary Ellen. The incident received little media attention after the initial report, suggesting that perhaps someone came forward with an explanation.

Frostbite, imagination, and fatigue were suggested as causes for Whidden's and Carroll's experiences on that frigid February night, but folks who knew Carroll back in Pictou believe the detective tapped Whidden to scare him. Then he lied about being touched on his own wrist and played up the creaks in the house as footsteps, just to keep the game going. It was the kind of thing Carroll would do, especially if he thought Whidden was susceptible, an elderly Pictou man said. Once it was reported in the newspaper as ghostly contact, there was no going back.

Nova Scotia's strong winds, including minor tornadoes, could whirl lightweight items from clotheslines, fences, wagons, and other outdoor sites; pin doors shut; and take away one's breath. The dogs said to be forerunners may have been the MacDonalds' real, live pet, a large black dog named Chief; or a little stray befriended by Mary Ellen. Given the community's heightened sensitivity to paranormal experiences, one dog sighting could start several stories. Richard Carroll's account of the horse that turned into a man in the spring of 1921 could be explained if Alex's horse had thrown him while he had ridden home from Antigonish that night. The horse and the man then went home, separately—one disappearing into the woods as the other entered the main trail from the narrow footpath—creating, for the men in the sleigh, the illusion of a horse turning into a man. They left no footprints because the snow had frozen rock hard—the very reason Carroll and his companions chose that particular day to

travel into the woods by horse and sleigh. They didn't return to look for footprints until some days later, when snow, sun, or rain could have erased any marks. (A horse that tosses its rider begs to be sold, and Alex sold his that spring.)

In his book, Richard S. Lambert cautioned against explanations that are more incredible than the events they try to explain. Any physical explanations of the strange events at the MacDonald farm depend as much on conjecture and coincidence as on fact, but are they any more incredible than ghosts? This much is true: The fires of 1922 happened, damaging the lives of the MacDonald family and their neighbours. The incident turned a happy home into a haunted place—if not by ghosts, then at least by the memory of one family's descent into misery.

"BALLAD OF CALEDONIA MILLS"

AUTHOR UNKNOWN

"Course, no one believes in bochdans, still you know it's very queer
That case down at Caledonia only twenty miles from here.
There's a house that catches fire, thirty-seven times a night
Was all printed in the papers, so of course it must be right."
Thus spoke Lizzie Ann McPherson at the dance at Donald Dhu's.
Lizzie Ann she takes the papers and keeps posted on the news.

[...]

"Mary Ellen in her nightie, but not meaning any harm,
Lit the fires, loosed the cattle, raised the devil on the farm.
Thirty-seven trips made Mary, lit the fires on the wall,
Yet the farmers who were watching didn't see the girl at all.
You see it was really Mary, yet it wasn't her at all,
Her subconscious self, they call it, lit the fires on the wall.
But if you ask this Mary Ellen, she will say without a doubt
That there are no bochdans in her. She wouldn't have the things about.
But of course this learned Doctor, this great man Professor Prince,
Must have reasoned with the spirits for there's been no fires since.
He's on speaking terms with bochdans, studied them at school in Rome."
Thus spoke Lizzie Ann McPherson, just before I took her home.

ACKNOWLEDGEMENTS

Special, personal thanks to N. Carroll MacIntyre, Archie Mills, Karen MacLeod, Lynn Gainer, Jocelyn Gillis, Joseph Graham, Dr. Erin Sullivan, Brian Inkster, Cathy Graham, Ronnie D. D. MacDonald, Cathleen MacKenzie, Laurinda Matheson, Anne-Marie Chisholm, Joe Morrison, Pat MacLean, Jane MacDonald, Charles Macdonald, Corinne Docker, Paul Kimball, Alison Hartson, Lewis MacKinnon, David Duggan, Andrea MacDonald, George Duggan, George White, Heather Mattie, Michael Linkletter, Steve MacLean, Deen MacIsaac, Joan Kuyek, Lois Peartree, Geralynn MacDonald, Sheila Hoegg, Doug Dort, Donna Davies, Darrell Walsh, Mary Guildford, Leah Skinner, and Caroline Cameron for your keen interest and help. Thanks are also due to the friendly and hospitable people at Caledonia Mills, Roman Valley, and Guysborough Intervale who supplied information on condition of anonymity: you know who you are!

I am grateful also to the clergy, employees, and volunteers of the Roman Catholic Diocese of Antigonish and its various parishes; the folks at Antigonish Heritage Museum and St. Francis Xavier University library and archives; Acadia University library and archives, the crew from Ruby Tree Films; staff at Hector Exhibit Centre, Nova Scotia Archives, Pictou-Antigonish Regional Library, Nova Scotia Office of Gaelic Affairs, Halifax Regional Police Service, Nova Scotia Fire Marshal's office, Greater Sudbury Public Library, Comhairle na Gàidhlig (The Gaelic Council of Nova Scotia); and the Sudbury District Branch of the Ontario Genealogical Society.

BIBLIOGRAPHY

Ancestry.ca. "Austin McGuire." www.ancestry.ca/cs/ca/census (accessed December 2011–March 2012).

Burlin, G. Scott. "An Examination of Juvenile Fire Setting and the Reasons that Kids Set Fires." Montgomery County Fire Marshal's Office, Conroe, Texas. January 2007.

Focus Adolescent Services. "Fire setting behavior and youth." focusas.com/firesetting.html (accessed March 2012).

Fraser, Dawn. "The Antigonish Ghost." *Cape Breton Mirror*, October 1953.

Fraser, Mary L. *Folklore of Nova Scotia*. Halifax: Nimbus Publishing, 1975.

Graham, Monica E. *The Great Maritime Detective: The Exploits and Adventures of the Notorious Peachie Carroll*. Halifax: Nimbus Publishing, 2009.

Graham, Monica E. *Historic New Glasgow, Stellarton, Trenton & Westville*. Halifax: Nimbus Publishing, 2012.

Lambert, Richard S. *Exploring the Supernatural: The Weird in Canadian Folklore*. Toronto: McClelland & Stewart, 1955.

Lowenstein, L. F. "The etiology, diagnosis and treatment of the fire-setting behaviour of children." *Child Psychiatry and Human Development* 19.3, 1918.

MacDonald, Alexander W. "Mystery at Caledonia Mills, Winter, 1921." Antigonish: Typewritten report of a conversation with Richard Carroll, 1984.

MacIntyre, N. Carroll. *The Fire-Spook of Caledonia Mills*. Antigonish: Sundown Publications, 1985.

Ryan, Judith. "Women's Unpaid Work: A Case Study of Coal Miners' Wives and Widows." Stellarton: Nova Scotia

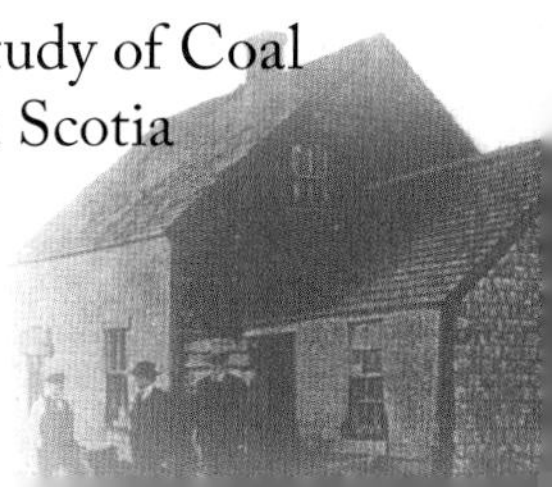

Museum of Industry, 1993.
Sherwood, R. H. *Maritime Mysteries*. Windsor: Lancelot Press, 1976.
Stanley-Blackwell, Laurie C. C., and R. A. MacLean. *Historic Antigonish: Town and County*. Halifax: Nimbus Publishing, 2004.
Wallace, Anne, and June MacDonald. *Glencoe: Sweet Memories*. Glencoe: n.p., 2004.
Walsh, Patrick: *The History of Antigonish*. Antigonish: Scotia Design Publications, 1989.
Whidden, Harold B. *My Experiences at the MacDonald Homestead, 1922*. Antigonish: Antigonish Heritage Museum and Pictou-Antigonish Regional Library digital collections, 2012.

PERIODICALS CONSULTED

Boston Globe, March 1922
Casket (Antigonish) January–July, 1922
Charlottetown Island Patriot, August 1917
Eastern Chronicle (New Glasgow), March 1922; March 1927
Halifax Herald, January–March, 1922
Halifax Sunday Leader, May 1922
Le Voyageur (Sudbury), 1977
Maclean's magazine, 1951
Montreal Standard, March 25 1922
New Glasgow Evening News, June 1922; August 1970
Pictou Advocate, January–July 1922
Sudbury Northern Life, 1981
Sudbury Star, June 1987

IMAGE CREDITS

Acadia University, Logan Collection of Canadiana 76
A. M. Chisholm 110
Antigonish Heritage Museum 3, 16, 37, 38, 44, 48, 49, 53, 55, 56, 59, 60, 64, 83, 86, 88
Archie Mills 8, 51, 69, 81, 90, 96, 102, 104
Carroll MacIntyre i, 19, 24, 26, 31, 34, 39, 65, 67, 71, 100, 108
George Dooley 14
Monica Graham iv, 1, 2, 13, 20, 85, 95, 112
Pictou Historical Photo Society 42, 78
Ruby Tree Films Inc., Halifax 91
St. Francis Xavier University 6, 82, 107
The Sudbury District Branch of the Ontario Genealogical Society 93

INDEX

I

J

K

L

M